designing
DVD
menus

How to create professional-looking DVDs

Michael Burns > George Cairns

with menu designs by Andy Potts

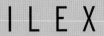

I L E X

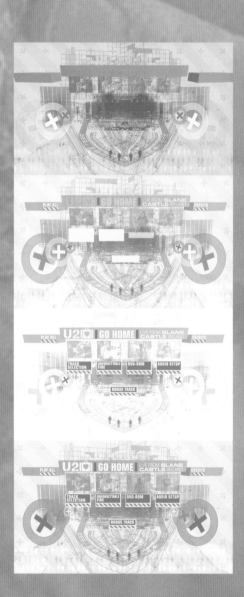

First published in the United Kingdom in 2004 by

ILEX
The Old Candlemakers,
West Street,
Lewes,
East Sussex,
BN7 2NZ
www.ilex-press.com

This book was conceived by
ILEX, Cambridge, England

ILEX Editorial, Lewes:
Publisher: Alastair Campbell
Executive Publisher: Sophie Collins
Creative Director: Peter Bridgewater
Editor: Stuart Andrews
Design Manager: Tony Seddon
Designer: Ginny Zeal
Artwork Assistant: Joanna Clinch

ILEX Research, Cambridge:
Commissioning Editor: Alan Buckingham
Development Art Director: Graham Davis
Technical Art Editor: Nicholas Rowland

British Library Cataloguing-in-Publication Data
A catalogue record for this book is available from
the British Library

ISBN 1-904705-42-1

Printed and bound in China

For more on designing DVD menus visit:
www.dvdmuk.web-linked.com

designing DVD menus

Contents

INTRODUCTION

Left: *The live-in-concert DVD has become an essential release for any major band following a big tour. When you have the capacity of DVD, you can do a lot more than simply present live footage.*

Above: *All the extras available on the DVD format need to be accessible via the menu.*

Above: *Accessibility isn't the whole story. It's vital that the design of a menu matches current branding, and ties up the package as a whole.*

DVD is the biggest technological success story of the last five years. As a means of distributing data, it is already stealing the mantle of the CD-ROM, but it's in the field of home entertainment that DVD has truly made its mark.

The advantages of DVD over video are easy to appreciate. Sharp picture quality and CD-quality digital surround sound have set DVD leagues ahead of VHS, and in terms of convenience and robustness, it's a more widely acceptable format than LaserDisc.

Multilingual subtitles and dubbing options enable a single disc to work across a much larger market, and the additional capacity of DVD means further bonus elements, such as supporting documentaries, outtakes, and feature-related footage, can be included to make the package even more attractive. DVD also gives you almost instant access to whatever point in a movie you wish to view. You don't need to rewind the tape or use a preview mode to find the point where you stopped watching: you simply select an option from a menu.

But the inclusion of all these powerful features means that the DVD needs a more complex interface than the video of old. VHS was simple – you inserted the tape and pressed play, or used fast-forward and rewind buttons to find a particular moment. With DVD, the extra options demand more capability than you can get from a few buttons. If the viewer needs to select from multiple audio tracks to listen to a commentary, wants to view the movie in an alternative language with or without subtitles, or wants to watch an alternative cut, then they need to be able to do so easily. This is where the DVD menu comes in.

The DVD menu

At its most basic, the DVD menu is simply a collection of buttons that allows a viewer to access the disc's contents. It can be as simple as a list of home movies, or as complex as a movie special edition, with optional scenes, commentaries, storyboards, and multiple camera angles. At the very least, it will usually include some form of scene access menu.

As a menu designer, you need to focus on two key issues: DVD menu structure, and the menu's physical layout. Your job is to make accessing the content as logical, intuitive, and enjoyable as possible. You need to decide on your menus and submenus, on what happens when the user reaches the end of a series of chapter buttons, and on how the user gets back to the main menu from a submenu buried three layers down.

Physical layout is as important. Not only do you need to make it clear, you also need to make it look like part of an overall package. Whether it's a major film, a personal wedding album,

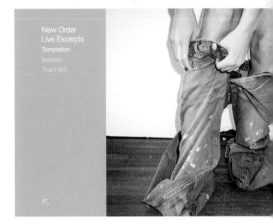

Right: Designs don't need to be complex to be effective. A combination of simplicity and minimalist style suits some subjects better.

Your job is to make accessing the content as logical, intuitive, and enjoyable as possible

or a pop-music video, the menu is the first thing a viewer will see when they insert the DVD into their player. It should make the viewer want to delve into the main feature, but also make them curious about any extras on offer.

It's easy to overlook the need to keep a balance between attractive design and usability. Unlike Internet or CD-ROM content, where you can anticipate a certain amount of knowledge and experience on the part of the end user, DVD is a mass medium that is enjoyed by the general public. What might seem logical and imaginative for a seasoned designer may be completely bewildering to your Aunt Mabel. Another factor to consider is that most people access a DVD using a remote control. It's easy to get around a website or a CD-ROM using a mouse, but a remote control is limited to four direction buttons and a return button. If you don't remember that at every stage of the design process, you're bound to make mistakes.

This book is here to help. We're going to run through the processes of putting together professional DVD

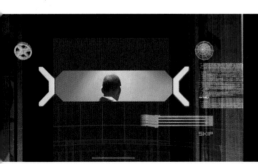

Below: *Super-slick transitions and special effects can make the DVD menu entertaining in its own right.*

Right: *Using existing designs and materials can save you time. What's more, it helps tie in the DVD with related releases in other media.*

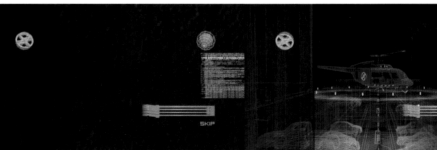

menus, covering every aspect from structure, to layout, to cool tricks that can bring a menu to life. More importantly, we will explore in-depth the thinking behind good DVD design. There's no substitute for experience, so we'll be taking tips from professional DVD menu designers – they've already encountered many of the problems you are likely to come up against in this new medium, and they know how to avoid or overcome them.

The DVD revolution

These days it isn't just the rich who can afford to produce and distribute DVD-video. You only need a basic digital camcorder and computer to shoot and edit footage, add titles and effects, then create and burn a working DVD. What's more, DVD menu design is being made easier all the time by a growing range of software titles.

The only downside of all this capability is that it's easy to let things get out of control. Lloyd Shaer, Creative Director for the successful London-based design studio The Pavement, compares it to the early days of desktop publishing:

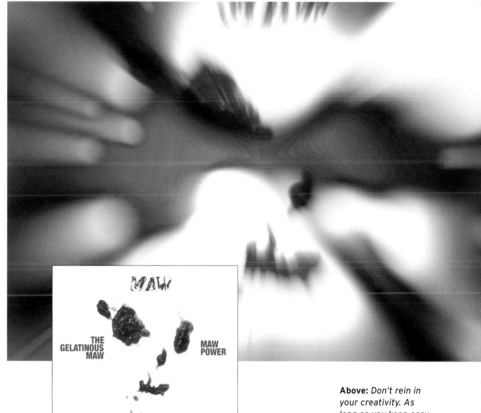

DVD is a mass medium that is enjoyed by the general public

Above: *Don't rein in your creativity. As long as you keep easy access in mind, your menu can be a playground in which to try out new ideas and techniques.*

Left: *The wedding DVD is rapidly replacing the wedding video. The menu should capture the mood of the day.*

Having access to the same means of production as the commercial design companies doesn't automatically mean that your product will look professional

Right and below right: *Maintaining a solid, consistent look and feel across several submenus is an essential part of DVD menu design.*

'When Macs came out, suddenly everyone was a designer. You had the same rubbish appearing all over.'

In other words, having access to the same means of production as the commercial design companies doesn't automatically mean that your product will look professional. A successful DVD menu still relies on design skills, and even experienced designers from other fields can have problems with the medium. Shaer explains:

'Designers used to specialize in one field. You could be a designer for packaging or the Web. With DVD, it's not like you're a jack-of-all-trades, but you do need a grounding in motion, layout, in design, and in sound. The guys we've got here at The Pavement are from backgrounds like print, TV graphics, animation, and even 3D, so everyone has a grounding in post-production of some kind.'

Right: *DVD menu design requires some competence in several disciplines. The designer may need to use image-editing and 3D applications as well as authoring programs.*

This book should help you develop some design skills of your own. What it isn't is a step-by-step guide to creating a complete DVD. We'll discuss doing particular tasks using particular applications, but we'll also keep things as generic as possible. If you understand how something works in one program, you should be able to apply what you have learned in another. We'll cover a range of products, from the low-end (Apple's iDVD and Pinnacle Studio) to the high-end professional packages (DVD Studio Pro and Adobe Encore) and run through some of the features that will help you to create DVD menus that present your content – whatever it may be – at its best. We'll also cover applications that enable the menu designer to create without relying on templates, such as Adobe Photoshop and After Effects.

The role of the menu

There's one theme we will keep coming back to, and that's the menu's role. The menu exists to provide access to the content on the disc. That doesn't mean that it can't be a showcase for your design skills, your technical genius, or your artistic vision, but this should all be secondary to access. In some cases, a sophisticated or deliberately arcane menu system suits the subject-matter of the movie, but not usually. Your menu's function is to present the content of the DVD. Yes, you want it to do this in an attractive and entertaining way, but when it comes down to it, it's the content that's most important.

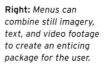

Right: *Menus can combine still imagery, text, and video footage to create an enticing package for the user.*

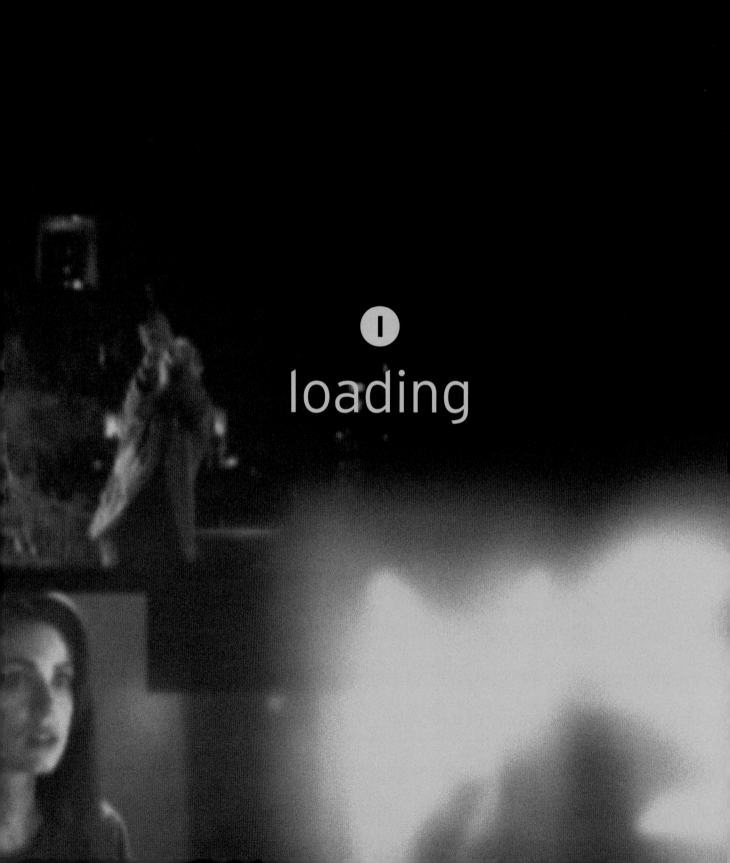

loading

What can you put on a DVD?

If you're one of the many who think that the V in DVD stands for video, prepare to be enlightened. DVD actually stands for Digital Versatile Disc, and the Versatile means it can store just about anything, as long as it's digital. There's a difference between DVD-ROM – the disc that you slot into your computer – and DVD-Video. DVD-Video conforms to a specification that means you can play the discs on a domestic DVD player, and this is the format we are focusing on in this book. While you may want to burn your own DVD-ROMs, or even include DVD-ROM content on your DVD-Videos, what we're concerned with here is building menus that work on standard DVD players.

Let's assume for now that there are three types of content you want your audience to access via your DVD menu. The first, obviously, is video. It may be the main film or a supporting feature, or it may be a video clip on a chapter selection screen or an animated transition.

The second type of content is audio. It may be packaged with the video as a soundtrack, or it may be one of a selection of 'behind the scenes' commentary tracks or foreign-language soundtracks.

Finally, we come to still imagery, which covers the menu layouts and buttons, and any imagery in the form of galleries, storyboard, etc.

As video is the most complex component, let's skip that for now and check out audio first.

Right: *Even amateur DVDs can have extras, including additional footage, interviews, and commentaries.*

Audio for DVD

The audio on a commercial DVD is normally encoded in several different formats, usually MPEG, Dolby Digital Stereo, and Dolby Digital 5.1 surround sound, and often the rival DTS 5.1 digital surround format. If you're using professional DVD authoring and sound- and video-editing software, you may also be working toward a Dolby Digital 5.1 or DTS disc, but you're more likely to be encoding for stereo. Your sources will be audio encoded with or dubbed onto your video, along with any additional background music or sound effects in WAV format (Windows), AIF (Mac), or MP3. In any case, you'll want the best quality. For most practical purposes, that means 44.1Khz CD-quality audio, or high-bit rate MP3s.

Importing images

Graphics are generally used as menu design elements to tie together the look and feel of the main film with the opening interface. Many people are

DVD-Video standards for NTSC and PAL

NTSC	PAL		
Interlaced fields	Interlaced fields		
59.94 fields per second	50 fields per second		
29.97 frames per second	25 frames per second		
720 x 480 pixels	720 x 576 pixels		
525 scan lines per frame	625 scan lines per frame		

content to use the stylish, although generic, graphics supplied with DVD authoring apps, but if you want to take your work to a professional level, then you'll need to create your own. Most professional DVD menu designers will use Adobe Photoshop (or something similar) to create these graphics, and professional authoring apps usually have support for Photoshop's native PSD file format – some even import layered PSD files. Otherwise, JPEG files are a fairly safe bet.

Commercial DVDs may also include photo slideshows, production design galleries, scripts, or storyboards. These are all graphics, too, and there's no reason why you can't supplement video content with still images if it will improve your product – most DVD authoring apps, regardless of level, include facilities for this.

You'll need to be aware of a few issues when creating your own graphics, and we'll come back to these from time to time throughout the book.

Video standards

Without video, a DVD would have little purpose, but video footage has to be prepared before it can be brought into your authoring software. Before you burn, you'll need to have finished working on your footage in your editing application, whether it's iMovie, Adobe Premiere Pro, or Final Cut Pro. In most cases, you will also have exported it in QuickTime, AVI, or MPEG-2 formats.

The other thing that you'll need is a clear idea of your DVD's target audience – different countries operate different television standards, and these are not compatible. NTSC is the standard for North America, Japan, and most South American and Pacific states. The European standard is PAL, also used in Australia, New Zealand, and parts of Africa. The table (*above left*) highlights the differences between the two.

Right: *Even this simple menu combines a mixture of still images (the background), audio (a soundtrack loop), and video footage (the chapter buttons).*

How do DVD menus work?

The rule 'content is king' certainly applies to DVD. Some DVDs are packed with extras and special features, and this bonus material may even have been the deciding factor in the DVD's purchase. But if content is king, then like any good ruler, it should be accessible to its subjects. A disc may contain truly excellent supporting material, but if the interface between the user and the content is badly designed, the user will be alienated and won't get the most from the disc.

Right: *DVD menus range from fairly simple front ends to more complex animated menus with sophisticated rollover graphics. DGP's menu for 24 is an example of the latter.*

© TCFHE Ltd.

The primary role of a menu is to enable the user to access content quickly and easily. This does not necessarily mean the design should be basic: if a designer creates a sophisticated-looking menu that complements the disc's content, then an audience is more likely to want to interact with it. Part of effective menu design, therefore, is to come up with a menu that matches the look and style of the movie. This marriage of print design and DVD design is hard to achieve, as Andy Evans, Managing Director from award-winning DVD design studio The Pavement, explains:

'The designer who supplies the DVD package design may also try to supply the menus. But in many cases, they fail to put any thought into how the menu will be used by the viewer. A designer is so used to making things look pretty. They hate the fact that you are restricted to using certain kinds of font, that you have to blur things so the menu doesn't

shake on TV. And everything's too small. Designers don't like to work in 1-bit. They are so used to being able to anti-alias stuff.'

Working with constraints

Designing for DVD is not like designing for the Web, or even CD-ROM. DVD is a surprisingly limited format when it comes to creating the interactive elements that Web and CD-ROM designers take for granted. Creating a sophisticated rollover button to work on a website, for example, is really a straightforward job. You take two different images and tell the browser

which image to display when the button is unselected, and which to display when the user selects the button. On a Web page, you can use a full-color bitmap image to represent both states, or even animate between them. This enables you to create moving button effects, such as a door opening or closing.

You can't create animated rollovers of this quality using DVD authoring packages. The limitations of the DVD format mean that rollover graphics are restricted to simple coloured shapes (called subpictures) that float above an onscreen button when it is selected. What's worse, because of the way the

DVD player overlays the subpictures on top of the background menu, you can't create them using full-colour graphics as you would if designing for the Web. The most you can achieve is a change of shape and opacity. Fortunately, there are ways to fight against the constraints that the DVD medium imposes on the designer, and we will be exploring these later in the book.

Below: *The supbictures were created using Photoshop's Custom Shape tool. It contains a library of presets that can easily be edited or combined.*

Right: *Part of a menu's character comes from the design of its subpictures. These subpictures were created for a DVD on extreme cycling.*

Right: *It's important that the style fits expectations, as in the art deco style of DGP's The Laurel and Hardy Collection menu.*

Below: *DGP were so keen to match the stop-motion style of Creature Comforts, they persuaded Aardman to build a model for them to animate as a menu.*

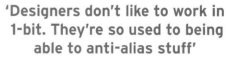

'Designers don't like to work in 1-bit. They're so used to being able to anti-alias stuff'

Andy Evans, Managing Director at The Pavement

DVD software

Up until the mid-1990s, amateur enthusiasts had to spend a small fortune to film, edit, and duplicate their own videos. The evolution and the increasing affordability of DV camcorders, along with the mass availability of personal computers powerful enough to edit video, has made it far easier to produce and distribute edited video and detailed still imagery on DVD. Today's creative professionals, and just about everyone else, can create a slick-looking DVD from the comfort of their own desktop computer.

Below: *Some packages, such as the affordable Pinnacle Studio, are aimed at the entry-level video editing and DVD authoring market.*

A variety of software packages vie for a cut of the DVD authoring market. As established players in the video-editing field, it's no surprise to see Adobe, Apple, and Pinnacle lead the way, and there are a variety of other DVD authoring applications on the Mac and PC platforms. The various packages are aimed at specific audiences and work in different ways. Each has its own strengths and weaknesses when it comes to menu design.

PC entry level: **Pinnacle Studio**

Pinnacle Studio is an affordable application aimed principally at home users. It is both a non-linear editing package and a DVD authoring package, meaning you don't need to jump between applications to create a finished product. Like all consumer-level packages, Pinnacle Studio is designed to help you get your videos onto DVD with the minimum of fuss, and it features a variety of pre-designed menu templates covering themes from birthdays to corporate presentations. Once you've chosen a template, you can edit it to give your DVD a unique look. Pinnacle Studio has a variety of differently styled menu buttons, which you can drag onto your menu to replace existing ones. You can then add stills or movie clips, and edit the menu's font and colours. All the buttons come with their own pre-designed subpictures, saving the novice the hassle of creating their own in a

Left: *Prosumer-level packages, such as Adobe Encore DVD, aim to grab the attention of designers with a mass of high-end authoring tools.*

The different functions of the Pinnacle Studio interface

Most of the DVD design functions are available in the Edit *tab*.

The Edit Menu *button* allows you to fine-tune your menu's fonts, images, and graphics.

Click the Capture *tab to digitize camcorder footage or import source material such as MOVs or AVIs.*

Like all DVD design applications, you can test your menu's looks and functionality before burning it to disc.

The color-coded Timeline *helps you see which sections of the movie relate to the different submenus (M1, M2, and so on).*

A menu's chapter markers are clearly flagged to match the colour of the relevant menu. Chapter return commands are indicated, too, to show in a visual way that the DVD will return to the appropriate menu when the video has finished playing.

third-party application, such as Photoshop, and overlaying them in the authoring package afterwards.

It's this level of automation that will deter serious designers from using Pinnacle Studio. Maintaining ease of use means there are limits to the control it offers over details like the shape of a subpicture and its opacity level.

Right: *Pinnacle Studio features an Album tab that holds many different templates, enabling you to design a usable menu with the minimum of fuss for your edited footage.*

Above: *iMovie is closely integrated with iDVD. The names you give to chapter markers in the editing package will be used to title the chapters in the authoring package.*

Mac OS entry level: **iDVD**

iDVD is part of Apple's iLife package, and works closely in conjunction with iMovie, Apple's entry-level video-editing program. Although these applications are technically separate, they work so closely together that they can be viewed as fully integrated, much like Pinnacle Studio, which houses its editing and authoring capabilities under one roof. You can edit your movie in iMovie, for example, and then add markers to indicate where each new scene on the DVD should begin. iMovie even features a *Launch iDVD Project* button, which transfers the edited footage and chapter markers straight to iDVD.

Once your edited footage has been imported into iDVD, you can bolt on menus using a selection of pre-designed templates, in the same way that you would with Pinnacle Studio. Likewise, you can alter font and button styles using a range of designs. The iDVD interface is very intuitive, allowing you to quickly customize existing templates by dragging images and movies onto areas in the iDVD workspace.

Getting to grips with iDVD

Select a theme for your imported movie from iDVD's library of Themes. Some of the themes contain motion menus, as indicated by the walking man icon. The library movies that feature in these motion menus can be replaced with your own footage to help customize the menu.

The Settings menu allows you to add transitions that will animate between a menu item as it is selected and the relevant chapter. These transitions include digital effects like Mosaic and Page Flip. A more ambitious designer would probably create animated transitions in a third-party application like After Effects, but for an easy-to-use quick package with fast results, iDVD is very effective.

The Media tab allows you to add assets like music from your iTunes library, and video clips from the Movies folder.

You can drag and drop stills directly from iPhoto into the iDVD interface. iDVD gives you the option of including the original photos on the disc as DVD-Rom material.

The motion menus loop until you get tired of seeing them. Turn them off by clicking on the icon so you can concentrate on customizing other aspects of the menu.

Left: *DVD Studio Pro gives you greater control of your menu's interactivity. You can adjust subpicture colour and opacity so that the user knows when a button is selected or activated.*

Other DVD applications

For this book, we've concentrated on only a few DVD-authoring programs – iDVD and DVD Studio Pro on the Mac, and Pinnacle Studio and Adobe Encore on Windows – but there are a few notable alternatives.

Ulead DVD Workshop: A competitor to Adobe Encore on the Windows platform, with an easy-to-use interface and support for a range of features for commercial DVD production, including advanced copy-protection, DLT and dual-layer DVD output, and 5.1 Dolby Digital audio support.

Pinnacle Impression DVD Pro: A fully-featured, prosumer-level authoring app from the creators of Studio and the highly regarded Liquid Edition editing package.

Sony Vegas+DVD Production Suite: Sony's professional level non-linear editor comes bundled with the DVD Architect authoring application, enabling the whole production process from one package.

Prosumer DVD software: DVD Studio Pro

Unlike iDVD, DVD Studio Pro allows you to get 'under the bonnet', giving you much more control over your design and authoring. You can add multiple language soundtracks, for example, and even get the disc to tell the DVD player which channel it should begin playing automatically – a useful option if you're creating a foreign language DVD.

DVD Studio Pro is template-based, and exploring the package's templates is a good way to start learning how the interface works. Once you get more confident with higher-end software, you can start creating more components outside of the authoring package. Creating menus in Photoshop, or moving menus in After Effects, will enable you to create a more unique looking menu.

Like other prosumer DVD authoring applications, DVD Studio Pro also lets you add your own subpictures, by creating any shape or symbol in Photoshop and overlaying it on your buttons in DVD Studio Pro. The authoring package also allows you to map different colours to your subpicture graphic to indicate what state it is in (whether it is activated). You can also edit the *Opacity* of the subpictures. This level of control is very useful when tweaking the finer details of your menu.

As with all Apple products, DVD Studio Pro is well integrated with other Apple applications. It reads chapter markers from iMovie and Final Cut Pro, and users of the latter applications will find the style of the DVD Studio Pro interface reassuringly similar. Unlike consumer-level applications, you can customize and save the workspace layout to suit your own way of working, which helps to streamline your workflow.

DVD Studio Pro allows you to get 'under the bonnet,' giving you much more control over your design and authoring

Additional software

The applications described previously enable you to design your DVD menu entirely within the authoring software. This is viable if you have a tight deadline, but there is the danger (as with any template-based application) that your menus will look similar to everyone else's. Professional designers prefer to create most of their menu design outside a DVD authoring package.

Right: *Adobe After Effects is a useful tool for the production of layered in-menu animations and animated transitions.*

Professional DVD menu designers operate in a similar way to Web designers, who will lay out the website in Photoshop first, creating rollovers and image maps, and then take the components through to a Web-authoring package in order to organize the links and HTML files. The DVD menu designer creates as much of the menu design as they can in a third-party application, then hands it over to someone else to deal with the authoring stage. This gives them total control over the look of a menu and the style of the buttons and subpictures.

Many professional menus feature motion elements that were created in Adobe After Effects. After Effects can be seen as a motion video version of Photoshop, enabling you to build up sophisticated animations by layering a variety of components. Take The Pavement's *Big Beach Boutique II* DVD, for example (see page 24). The main menu constitutes a looping animation of a beach, with people

Right: *Photoshop is as much used in DVD menu design as it is in Web design and print publishing. Menu elements and layouts are created first in Photoshop and then imported into a DVD authoring package.*

'If you're going to use 3D, you need to use it properly.'
Lloyd Shaer, Creative Director at The Pavement

dancing, floating boats, and a telescope in the foreground that holds the disc's navigation options. Each component was filmed separately and then layered together in After Effects. An authoring application was then used to link the animated menus to the disc's content, adding subpictures and subtitles and encoding the final product.

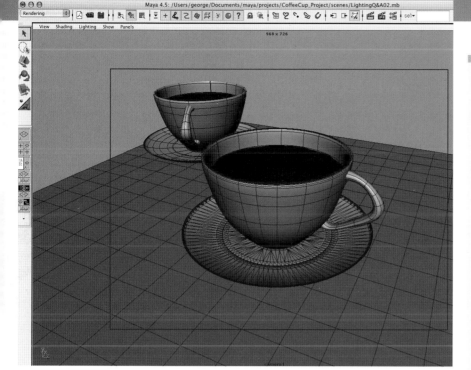

Maya File Edit Modify Create Display Window Lighting/Shading Texturing Render Paint Effects Help

Maya 4.5: /Users/george/Documents/maya/projects/CoffeeCup_Project/scenes/LightingQ&A02.mb

Rendering

968 x 726

View Shading Lighting Show Panels

VIDEO EFFECTS
Create moving transitions to add flair to your menu

A DVD can be given extra depth and polish with animated transitions that play when a menu item is selected. It's also common to preface a disc with a short introductory sequence featuring a montage of footage from the movie, as this can add a sense of excitement and anticipation. Packages like After Effects and Adobe Premiere Pro feature a variety of special effects filters that can help you stylize your short introductory montage. You can reduce the colour of the images, warp them, or even re-time them to play in slow motion. Premier Pro also has a Title Designer, enabling you to create animated captions that give your introduction sequence a true Hollywood feel.

If you do create an introductory movie or have clips from the DVD playing in the background of the main menu, be careful not to spoil the viewer's enjoyment of the film by giving away key plot details.

SOUND EFFECTS
Add audio to give your menu punch

Audio is a crucial part of every killer DVD menu. Many of the professionals we spoke to while writing this book stressed the role sound can play in adding an extra level of depth and detail to the user's experience. For example, *Bowling for Columbine*'s DVD menu is largely a still graphic. It appears more sophisticated because of the looping sound effect of a bowling alley. You can download many sound effects from the Web for free, but check for copyright messages first. .Mac users can download a free range of iMovie sound effects from www.mac.com. While many templates in entry-level authoring applications come with pre-scored music, budding musicians can create their own using Apple's Garage Band. Adobe has its own program, Audition, which features sampled loops that can be strung together and layered to create a unique backing track. Sound effects and music can also augment transitions, which play when the user selects a menu item.

3D or not 3D?

Some menus feature sophisticated 3D environments that provide an animated interface. 3D is useful for augmenting your 2D elements with, for example, flying logos. It can also be used to create entire menu interfaces. To design a menu for children's classic TV show *Stingray*, design company The Pavement created a 3D model of the *Stingray* submarine's interior to use as the main menu interface.

The Pavement's Creative Director, Lloyd Shaer, worked on the project, but offers a word of caution to people not yet experienced with 3D applications like Maya and 3ds max: 'To be honest, I don't think there's a huge call for 3D. If you're going to use 3D, you need to use it properly. If you rush it and don't do quality rendering, it won't look convincing. Some people get discs done using people who have not been properly trained in that area, which is a mistake.'

Above: *Packages like Alias's Maya 6 can be used to create graphics for your menu by using 3D modeling tools. You can create animated transitions from your models by introducing a virtual camera that seems to fly around the 3D environment.*

Digital assets

As a menu designer, you need to think carefully about what you intend to put on your disc, whether it's movie clips, soundtracks, or background stills, before you put your menu together. Award-winning design company The Pavement have been creating cutting-edge DVDs for years. Co-founder Lloyd Shaer describes how the professionals go about identifying and organizing their DVD's assets at the pre-production stage:

Below: *The music video Big Beach Boutique II features a variety of assets, including games, songs, and stills of the fans taken at the event.*

The Pavement
The Pavement wins awards for its beautifully designed discs, which feature effective yet innovative navigation options. They have continued to 'push the envelope' when designing menus that take advantage of the functionality of the DVD medium. Check out the showcases for *My Little Eye* (see page 152) and *Fat Boy Slim: Big Beach Boutique II* (see page 180) to see how The Pavement's designers approached the task of creating menus to suit very different content – a thriller DVD and a music DVD.

'We meet with the client and begin by creating a long wish list. In this first meeting, everything comes out onto the table', explains Lloyd. 'Next we sift through it all and start to collate what we've got. Then we go away from the meeting and pick the team that's going to work on the disc.

We work out what is pertinent to the disc and what is important to the user. You start to get the shape of the various compartments that make up the menu. You might have a room with a feature in it, a room with extra content, some of it might be ROM, some of it might be stills, some of it might be archive footage –

TERROR IN THE SKY

1. 5,4,3,2,1... 2. THE EVIL HOOD

3. THE NEW FIREFLASH 4. FIRST EMERGENCY

MENU NEXT

Left: *Abbey Road Interactive's design for the* Thunderbirds *series DVD utilized key assets from the series along with specially created elements made to match the style. The resulting menu is fun to interact with, but maintains clarity along with a consistent look and feel for the product as a whole.*

it all depends on whether it's a music, film, or TV DVD. Your rooms get filled up with all these assets. Then you can sit and look at them and see correlations between them.'

Once your potential assets have been identified and compartmentalized, the disc will start to take shape. 'It's like when you wake up in the morning and everything's hazy, then you get to that point when everything becomes very clear. You know who the artist is and you know the fan base. You know your audience. You know what your budget is. You know what content is important to the disc and what content isn't.'

Only once the assets have been identified and organized into submenus will Lloyd and his team turn their attention to the cosmetic side of the menu. 'Once it's all laid out, we sit down and try to come up with a clever idea that's easy to work with but is interesting for the user to interact with.'

Stay focused

Every menu has a primary function, and whatever assets a disc may contain, the designer needs to stay focused on that purpose. Lloyd has a clear idea of what a DVD designer's role is: 'You are creating a menu. A lot of people forget that that is all they are creating. At the end of the day, it is only a menu. When you go into a restaurant you want to see what you are going to eat. If you can't, then what's the point?'

Lloyd believes that designing an overly complex menu is the fault of inexperience. 'Everyone's guilty of going too far and making their menu too difficult. You grow up. A lot of new people are coming into DVD design. The 'designer' who's asked to do the menu might just happen to be friendly with the artist or friendly with the label or know someone who knows someone. Very often they forget that the viewer will be looking at the menu on a TV. You could

be sitting two feet from that menu or you could be sitting fourteen feet away. You could be looking at a widescreen TV or a portable TV. You might wear glasses; you might be old, you might be young – the would-be designer doesn't take any of that into consideration. He or she sits in front of the PC screen, a foot away. They make nice, dinky little buttons. When they sit back, they can't see a thing! I make the guys here at The Pavement step back, even after all these years. I grab their chair and pull them back and say 'Can you see it? I can't!' From where I sit in the office, I can see all the screens from afar. If I can't see a menu clearly then it doesn't work. It's a litmus test. If I don't think a menu works, it doesn't go anywhere.'

It's easy to get carried away with the aesthetics of menu design and the logistics of linking the various menus together. It cannot be said often enough that the menu's job is to serve the user. Lloyd has the last word: 'As long as you can get to where you want to go quickly and easily, you've got a successful DVD. The moment that a user gets lost, or they can't see a subpicture, they can't read what they are looking at, or they can't go anywhere, or it fails in the player, then you haven't got a successful DVD. It's as simple as that.'

Showcase

Laurel and Hardy - The Collection

Sometimes a menu layout has to be adaptable to cover a whole series of DVDs, as the design work on *Laurel and Hardy – The Collection* demonstrates.

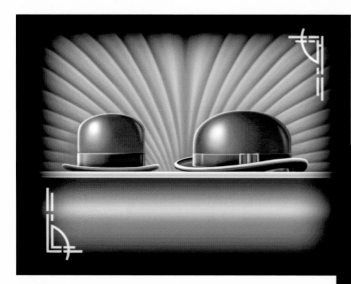

Left: *The Art Deco fan used as the background of the menu was taken from early promotional material.*

Below: *The main menu was designed to present content for a variety of different discs. As everything was on layers, it was a straightforward job to change the video clips and text for each disc in the box set.*

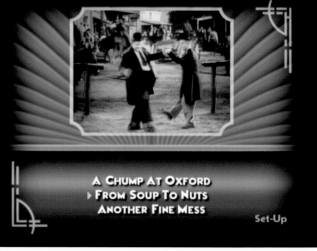

A CHUMP AT OXFORD
▸ FROM SOUP TO NUTS
ANOTHER FINE MESS

Set-Up

'We designed our own brief to see if the client would go with it'

When Universal decided to release the ultimate *Laurel and Hardy – The Collection* in a 21 disc DVD box set, they turned to design company DGP to create a menu that would easily adapt to suit a wide range of features and short films. We spoke to DGP designer Tim Long to see how the design of the Laurel and Hardy DVD menu evolved. We began by asking him what kind of brief he had.

'As with many of these things, we didn't really get a brief. We designed our own brief to see if the client would go

with it. When we looked at their product we said we thought it should be something classy rather than overtly quirky and convinced them that that's what they wanted. We don't get this kind of creative freedom when the talent is still alive, but obviously Laurel and Hardy weren't around to say 'yeah' or 'no!''

Tim designed a template that could be used across the whole collection. This constrained his menu design, as it had to suit a large number of discs, each varying in terms of content, but it needed to be done. 'If we'd got into some sort of non-formulaic design that changed for every disc across the 21 discs in the

'When you get a font on TV, if you've got a couple of pixels between the gap on the E, it's going to completely disappear'

Left and below: *To link the disc and packaging together, the artist who drew the DVD's cover illustration also illustrated the Laurel and Hardy characters for the menu's introduction sequence.*

collection, we'd be working on it for months. From a business point of view, you have to reduce the time spent on it. Most of the budget is chewed up on encoding and proofing the discs.'

The main menu was split up into sections. 'We made a division on the menu screen so we could get the quarter screen movie cut in for the main menu. We wanted to have a consistent area for the navigation options so the Art Deco fan and the horizontal line is in the same place throughout the disc. In actual fact, it was a bit of a squeeze to fit text on a few of the menus because, as is often the case, they hadn't refined the content. They were pulling it in from all over the place and finding out what they could legally get hold of. For some menus, they didn't know they'd got the content until the eleventh and a half hour. On one of the 21 discs, they trumped up a couple of extra movies at the last moment, which made the text in the menu really tight.'

It was important that the design of the Laurel and Hardy menu matched the design of the packaging. 'So often what we get as DVD designers is effectively something that could have been print designed and has to be adapted to DVD. Quite often with a movie you look at the sleeve design and it doesn't reflect the movie. In terms of producing a product that is cohesive with the menus, it doesn't always hang together. To make the Laurel and Hardy menu and packaging complement each other meant collaborating with the print designers to create elements that could be used in both. To work hand in hand with the print designers in this way is quite unusual. I laid out the constraints of what we needed for the menus and said it would be really great if it could tie in with the actual box set packaging.

Left: *For* Laurel and Hardy: The Collection, *menu designer Tim Long worked closely with print designer Daren Thienel and artist Simon Williams to create a product that had a single, consistent look.*

Reusing components

The Laurel and Hardy menu features some iconic Art Deco style symbols.

'In the top righthand corner, you'll notice there's an 'H' in the symbol. And in the bottom lefthand corner, you've got an 'L'. I explained to the print designer that he had to work within the title safe area (*see page 69-71*). If you look at the main menu, those two bits of Art Deco paraphernalia (the L and the H) mark the edge of the title safe constraint. They provided a good visual way for the print designer to know what would look good on a TV screen.'

As well as working with print designers and illustrators, Tim had to liaise with video editors to make sure the movie clips fitted into the ornately shaped window in the menu. 'The menu was designed in Photoshop. I supplied the mask and the picture frame and the background for the Avid editors to use. They did a montage of clips, got the edit approved, then resized the edit to fit inside the frame.'

The mask that Tim provided for the non-linear editors to use was an alpha channel that had a soft mix between

Otherwise you look at the packaging, buy the box set, stick the DVD on, and think 'hang on, this has been designed by someone else.'

To find the right fonts, Tim gave a print design co-worker some rough illustrations for the layout of the menu and explained the need to find fonts that would suit the DVD medium. The print designer came up with a selection of fonts, which Tim tested out on a TV. He wanted a real period font to go with the Art Deco background, but the choice was constrained by the need to fit all the episode information on the menu and still keep the text legible.

We asked Tim if he thought that, generally speaking, print designers understand the limitations of designing for DVD and the low-resolution TV screen. 'In TV, you're working to 72 DPI and in print, you're working to around 300 dpi upward. I don't think designers for print understand that when a font is on TV, a couple of pixels between the gap on the E will completely disappear and become a splodge. With the majority of the jobs we get, we are sent the print work to adapt. The titles they come up with are often bright reds, which look great in print, but on TV they fight and wobble all over the place. So we have to come to a compromise with what the print guys might want.'

'There was a danger that the subpicture would not have been noticeable so we added the subtle colour'

white and black. This allowed the edges of the video clip to mix gently with the background illustration, which helped to anchor the motion video elements with the still components that made up the rest of the menu.

The only colour aspects of the Laurel and Hardy menu are the subpictures, indicating what option has been selected. We asked Tim if he was ever tempted to keep the whole menu monochrome.

'I was tempted, but there was a danger that the subpicture would not have been noticeable so we added the subtle colour. It's a kind of minty, greeny blue that featured in some of the later, colour movies. The colour was taken from the cards that introduced the movie. The DVD has the kind of menus which make it pretty obvious what you are choosing so we didn't need subpictures that were too elaborate.'

Although Tim has created the text for the 21 discs in the collection, his job as a designer isn't necessarily over. 'It's possible I may have to re-version the menus. I think they're going to put the box set out in Europe so I'm going to have to redo captions like 'Play black and white version' in French or German. We did ask up front if it was going to go out in Europe and needed translation, but they weren't sure at that point.

As a designer, I like to know because then you allow that little bit more room in the menu.'

Tips from the top

In what is still a relatively young medium, Tim Long can be considered a veteran designer. There's no substitute for hard-earned experience, so we took the opportunity to squeeze out some last nuggets of DVD design knowledge from him before he got back to work on his next commercial project.

First we asked him to give an overview of the DVD design experience.

'In a way, DVD is quite easy to design for in terms of placing stuff on the screen. You've got very specific constraints anyway. In terms of getting all the detail of it designed, like clipping sounds and nice loops on motion menus, it's a case of trial and error, and a lot of experimentation.'

What does Tim know now that he wished he had known when he first started designing for DVD?

'I wish I'd realized that most DVD players don't meet the specification of DVD, so they don't behave as you expect them to behave. As the market grew and more players came into the market place, we had more players to trial our menus on to see what would work and what

wouldn't. We hit the initial problem, like the Matrix, of people turning around and saying 'my player doesn't play it'. Some DVD players still have trouble playing a clip under one second. The shortest clip that I've used is 25 frames and there was an issue because they had to encode it for longer, then clip it down in authoring. If you've only got a second of movie and you're taking out 8 frames for audio on that, it doesn't really leave you with anything. As a lot of the encoders won't actually encode under 3 seconds, you should stick to making transitions a minimum of 3 seconds

'As the years go on, you refine your designs because you get to know what looks good on TV. I guess the main thing is to find out early if your design looks good on a poor TV, as this may be what it is ultimately viewed on.'

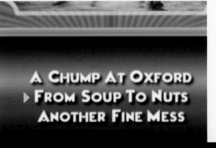

Left: *The simple subpictures were designed to fit in with the menu's elegant style. Making them colour against monochrome helped ensure that the menu's user could navigate through the content with ease.*

Right: *The ornate Art Deco symbols (the L bottom left and the H top right) do more than add decoration to the menu. They also help the designer make sure the appropriate content will be visible on any TV monitor.*

2

menu basics

Building and customizing menus
Working with templates in entry-level applications

DVD authoring applications like Apple iDVD and Pinnacle Studio make DVD menu creation a straightforward and enjoyable experience. They are designed to enable novice users to put a menu together as quickly and easily as possible and, with this in mind, they rely heavily on pre-designed templates covering a range of popular themes. All you need to do to create a fully functional DVD menu is import your video and source images into the package, then drag and drop your DVD components into the template.

*Below right: As much as you might appreciate Apple's stylish template design, you probably don't want to leave the company's logo on every menu. Select iDVD > **Preferences** and untick the Show Apple logo watermark option to get rid of it.*

Building menus in iMovie and iDVD

iDVD works in close concert with its iLife partner, iMovie. Editing in the latter, you can place chapter markers then – once the movie is complete – launch an iDVD project containing all the assets at a click of a button.

Once launched, iDVD takes a template-based approach. The good news is that its templates, or 'Themes', can be quite sophisticated, with video clips playing in the background, looping music, and transitions. The current version includes 44 themes (although some are just variations) covering weddings, birthdays, holidays, touring, and other family topics, along with some useful theatrical and cinematic themes. If you have a tight deadline, this approach can really speed things up. Take a pre-designed wedding theme, slot in the video and any audio or still images, then personalize, and you can have a slick DVD in under an hour. Additional theme collections are also available.

A typical template

The Settings section relates to menu elements like text. The colour of the text complements the colours used in the theme to keep the look consistent.

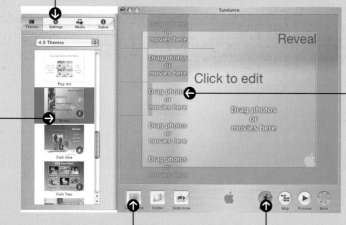

Sections such as this within the template – called Dropzones – are editable. You can personalize them by editing the text, or adding movies or images.

Scroll down the list of themes to find a template suitable for your DVD's content. Apple add more themes with each new release of iDVD.

iDVD's Customize icon opens a sliding drawer, enabling you to browse through the program's gallery of themed menu templates.

Some menus have an animated element, as indicated by the walking man icon. You can turn off moving elements in an animated menu by clicking on this button.

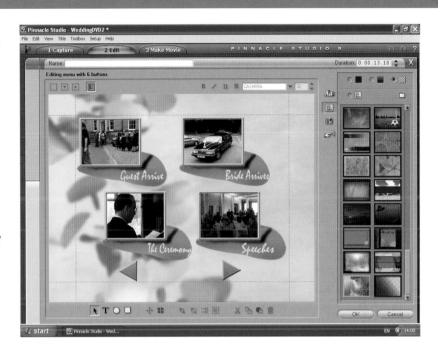

Right: *Pinnacle Studio incorporates video-editing and DVD authoring in a single working environment.*

Using Pinnacle Studio

If you work on a PC, you can take a similar approach in Pinnacle Studio. Pinnacle Studio combines non-linear editing and DVD design so that they are both 'under one roof', making it easy to tweak the content of your DVD and design a suitable menu at the same time. Like iDVD, Studio features a wide selection of pre-designed menu templates into which you can slot your content. These contain the usual family and holiday themes, plus a few fun variations, but the range also includes some more business-oriented designs.

Editing

Before you design a menu, you need to get your movie into shape. Even if you're doing nothing more than creating a compilation of home movies, editing is important, as it enables you to remove unnecessary or tedious footage and patch over bad camera work and poorly recorded sound.

Presentation of your carefully edited work is just as important. Your DVD movie content may well be edited with high production values, but a poorly designed and confusing menu may lead the user to presume that the content is equally poor.

One advantage of using iMovie and iDVD or Pinnacle Studio is that it's so easy to switch from video-editing to DVD authoring and back again. While this wouldn't be an important feature in a professional workflow, it can be a useful facility for amateur users looking to capture family memories on DVD.

Working with templates in Pinnacle Studio

You can click on a menu template to preview the design in the main editing window and get a sense of its suitability for your disc's content.

Once you've imported and edited your footage, click on Studio's Show Menus tab to access a variety of themed menu templates.

To access the pre-designed templates in Pinnacle Studio, you need to be in Edit mode.

Click on the page turn arrows to access the full range of templates available.

Some templates contain a moving component like an animated background, as indicated by this icon.

The edited footage is currently being displayed in Storyboard mode. You can click here to change the footage to a more traditional timeline that will enable you to see the parallel tracks of sound and video.

Customizing menus

Customize iDVD's themed templates to create a unique DVD menu

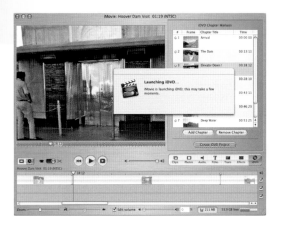

1 Once you've edited your raw footage in iMovie and added music and chapter markers, you're ready to click on the *Launch iDVD* button. This will open up iDVD and create a new project containing your edited video. iDVD will also pick up the chapter settings you defined in iMovie and automatically label the chapters with the names you gave them.

Looping Movie

As 'icing on the cake' edit a montage of highlights from your video to play as a looping movie within the DVD interface. The maximum length of the loop in iDVD is just under 30 seconds, so tailor your sequence to fit that duration.

2 Click on the *Customize* icon and browse through the pre-designed themes available. Pick the one that most suits your content. For this example, we went for Reveal, which features motion elements. The main animated element is a looping movie, which runs in the background, but it also features animated buttons that wipe or fade-in to frame. This gives the menu some visual excitement.

3 To customize this default menu theme, add your own images. Go to the *Media* icon. To add an image, select the pull down window and choose *Photos*. This will take you straight to your Mac's iPhoto library. Here you can choose any image from iPhoto and drag it onto the area of the screen where it says 'Drag photos or movies here'.

Image sources

You can customize your DVD menu interface using screenshots taken from your movie. Alternatively, scan in some shots from your photo album or download them from your digital camera and import them into iDVD.

4 For more motion, try adding a movie of your own to the themed menu. Go to *Media* and choose *Movies* from the pop-up window. This gives you access to any movies or iMovie projects stored in the Mac's Movie folder. Simply drag the desired movie or project onto the main iDVD window and a 30-second looped sequence will play in the large area on the right behind the menu options.

Customizing menus

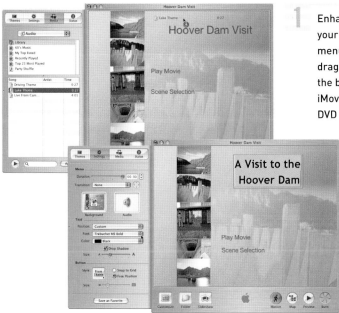

1 Enhance the experience of the DVD user by adding music to your menu. Go to *Media* and select *Audio* from the pull down menu. Select any piece of music from your iTunes library and drag it to the main iDVD window. The sound will then play in the background. iDVD is seamlessly integrated with iPhoto, iMovie, and iTunes, enabling you to add any assets to your DVD quickly and easily.

2 By default, the title of your DVD menu will be the name you gave to the iMovie project. To change it to something more appropriate, simply click on the text in the iDVD menu window and type in something new. You also change the *Font*, *Size*, and *Color*. We went for Trebuchet to reflect the style of the '30s when the Hoover Dam was built, and ticked the *Drop Shadow* box to help the title stand out.

3 Every TV screen is different, so there's a danger that some of your text will be unreadable, if it appears outside the viewable area of screen used by some of the DVD's audience. To prevent this, go to iDVD's *Advanced* menu option and choose *Show TV Safe Area*. A red box on screen will define which parts of the menu can safely contain text and clickable buttons. Drag the text into this safe area.

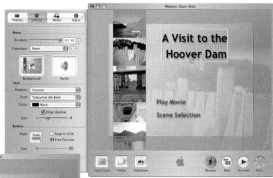

4 You can turn the default text into a variety of shaped buttons using the *Settings* menu – click on the *Style* icon to browse. We chose a cool, TV-shaped icon for our clickable buttons. We added a movie to the Play Movie button and a still image to the Scenes button. Use the *Size* slider in the *Button* menu to reduce the size of your icons so the menu doesn't look overcrowded. Simple and sparse often works better than a busy menu.

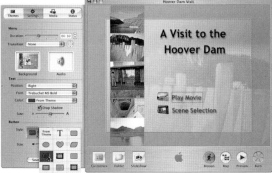

Text design

If you add any extra text to the menu, make sure that it fits in with the overall design of the interface. Go to *Settings* to choose your text's alignment, font, and size. The colour of the text will automatically complement the theme you have chosen, but you can override this if you would prefer it to match any of the components you have added.

Customizing menus
Reworking Pinnacle Studio's themes to create a different style

1 To access the DVD menu templates go to *Album* in the menu bar and choose *Disc Menus*. Browse through the menu options to find the designs most suited to your DVD's content. Drag the selected menu template from the album to the beginning of the *Timeline* to apply it. Don't let the software automatically create a chapter for each shot as you'll be creating your own chapters later.

2 For greater control over menu creation, display the edited clips as parallel tracks of video and sound instead of a storyboard of consecutive clips. This makes the interface behave like a more high-end DVD package, giving you more control over the menu design. Any motion menu movies will appear in the *Video Track*. Buttons and chapter graphics will be overlaid on the *Title Track*. In the *Menu Track*, you'll see M1 for Menu 1.

3 Double-click on the *DVD Menu* thumbnail in the timeline to edit the design. Our wedding menu example has one of those ornate fonts that are so typical of the genre. As intricate fonts like this are hard to read from a distance, limit the amount of buttons on each screen so that you can keep the text relatively large. You can also experiment with plainer fonts, although a real-life couple may want to stick to the ornate version.

4 Like iDVD, Studio has a wide selection of customizable buttons. You can also import stills or screen grabs from the video to make the menu more unique. Any images can easily be scaled and positioned to fit the template buttons. Here we've customized a template to create main menu links to two separate submenus, each with their own chapter selections.

Customizing menus

1 Pre-designed template menus attempt to short cut the design process by doing everything for you, but you'll need to do lots of editing to tailor the template to suit your DVD's specific needs. Studio's default buttons come with subpictures that automatically change colour to indicate a button's state, when selected or activated by the menu user. In this example, the active colour assigned by Studio is green. You can easily change the subpicture's highlight colour to complement your overall colour palette.

2 Use your own images as part of a design to make the template feel less generic. Choosing a still image and a background that complements the button layout will create a sense of balance.

Feedback

After spending hours tweaking a DVD template, you may find it hard to be objective. Show your design in progress to a friend, as they will have a fresh perspective. They'll be able to point out any design flaws you may have missed (and spot the odd spelling mistake!).

3 As TV screens vary in size and resolution, avoid creating buttons in the danger areas at the edge of the menu. If some TV owners can't access a menu because the button they need is off their screen, you will soon get complaints. Studio automatically displays a dotted red line to indicate the safe area for positioning your buttons.

4 Don't let the templates lead your designs. You don't have to limit yourself to using templates called 'Wedding' when making a wedding DVD. Experiment with some of the other template designs to see if you can modify them to suit your design needs. This template combines a warm colour palette with a legible font to make an attractive alternative to traditional wedding DVD design.

Connecting menus
Connecting your menus should be a painless process

Once you've customized your DVD interface by adding text, images, and movies to an existing iDVD template (or theme), it's time to make sure everything is connected in a way that will make it easy for the user to navigate around the disc's content. DVDs may get watched on many occasions over the years, so it's important that the viewers can find the bits they want quickly, without having to do lots of picture searching.

Below left: *iDVD automatically creates linked and labeled scene menus based on the chapter markers made in iMovie.*

Slideshow
The *Slideshow* button creates a *Folder* that links to a special submenu. The DVD designer can drag in photographs to the folder from iPhoto, set the duration of each image and even add transitions. The slides can be triggered manually by using the DVD remote control, and you can also add an audio file to accompany the images.

As we have discussed, you can create and label DVD chapter (or scene) markers when you edit your film in iMovie. This enables you to divide up your finished work into scenes, and gives you a chance to pick out the moments that your audience will want to keep coming back to.

When you launch an iDVD project from within iMovie, all your chapters are placed inside the iDVD *Scene* menu that appears in the main menu, with each scene bearing the label you gave it in iMovie. You can edit these labels once you start working in iDVD by selecting them and typing in alternative text.

Choosing chapters
When choosing chapters, consider the constraints of your software. iDVD limits you to a maximum of 12 chapters (or scenes) per page. Depending on the template (or theme) that you have chosen, iDVD will automatically create multiple menu pages and break these scenes down into sets. To help you

Relabeling text
Rename any text links to various scenes or chapters by double-clicking on them and editing them as you would using a word-processing package. To relabel a submenu *Folder's* text, click on it once (if you click twice it will take you to the submenu).

Disabling motion
iDVD allows you to disable any motion menus while you fine tune the menu design. This gives your computer's processor less work to do, and so makes the application run more smoothly. You can do this by clicking on the *Motion* icon. Make sure you re-activate the motion menus before you click Burn, or they will be forever static on your finished disc.

navigate around the DVD's content, the application also creates icons to take you to the next set of scenes or back to the main menu. You can customize each chapter set menu by dropping in a different image, so differentiating one page from the next. This will add a sense of variety to the menu as well as help the user recognize which chapter set they have selected.

Connecting menus together in iDVD

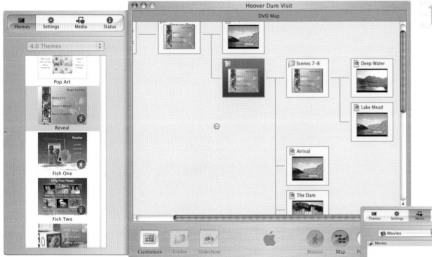

1
Like higher-end DVD authoring applications, iMovie 4 can give you a visual representation of your DVD's contents and their relationship to each other. Click on the *Map* icon and you'll be taken to the *DVD Map*: a tree-based graphic describing your menu hierarchy. It's a useful way of understanding how each submenu links to the main menu. Annoyingly, you can't expand the iDVD window to see the whole 'tree' in one go – you need to scroll around the window if you want to see everything.

2
You can add new chapters to the existing submenus within iDVD itself. Simply select the relevant submenu page, then go to *Media*, select *Movies*, and drag a movie thumbnail onto the main iDVD menu window (although you need to avoid any Dropzones, or you will merely replace the movies used there). To edit the order the chapters play, drag the text links up and down in the main window.

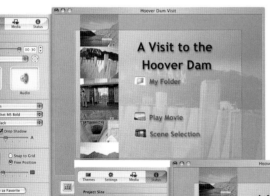

3
In our Hoover Dam example, the main menu links to two submenus (one containing Chapters 1-6 and a second featuring Chapters 7-9). These submenus are contained inside iDVD folders. You can create additional links to new submenus by clicking on the folder icon. Customize the folder's icon by adding images or movies to it. Click on it to go to the new submenu you have created, then add content (such as extra video, audio, or a photo slideshow).

4
As you progress with your menu design, keep tabs on the size of the project to make sure you don't exceed the DVD's storage capacity. iDVD 4 has a useful *Status* pane that shows you how much of the disc you have filled. You can also see how many minutes of motion menus you have left.

Navigation in Pinnacle Studio
Automatic override: taking control of the design process

Before we link our menus together, a word of caution. As an entry-level package designed for the domestic user, Pinnacle Studio likes to do everything for you. It will even offer to edit the video for you by randomly selecting clips of footage and editing them to a chosen music track. No serious editor would contemplate letting a machine edit their footage, and a serious DVD designer needs to be aware that Pinnacle Studio's automatic functionality extends to making the DVD interactive. If you want more control, you need to be wary of what it will try to do for you, such as place a chapter marker at the beginning of each shot and offer to make the DVD return to the main menu after each chapter has been played. As most DVD users will want to watch video as an uninterrupted narrative, it's very unlikely that you'd want the DVD to go to the main menu at the end of each chapter, so set and link your chapters manually.

So far, we have a series of video clips and some customized menu designs. These separate elements now need to be carefully and logically linked together in a way that makes it easy for the user to access the disc's content.

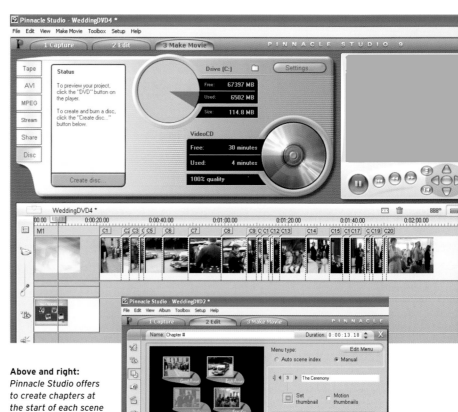

Above and right:
Pinnacle Studio offers to create chapters at the start of each scene automatically. Just say no and check the 'Don't ask me this again' box. You need to take control of the way your DVD is linked together.

Changing button thumbnails
Pinnacle Studio automatically uses the first frame of a chapter to create a *Preview* icon for certain types of button. You can use the *Toolbox* to grab a different frame for these previews. Click on the *Motion Thumbnails* icon to add a looping video preview. These small details add an extra level of quality and detail to the look of your disc.

Connecting menus in Pinnacle Studio

1 When you add a template motion menu to the *Timeline*, the interactive buttons are overlaid on the *Title* track. You can choose a different video clip to give the menu a unique look. Simply drag the button thumbnail in the *Title* track to overlap on a new clip in the *Video* track. This clip will become part of the menu and will loop. Drag any submenus to the timeline before linking them to chapters.

2 To make a menu interactive, double-click on the thumbnail in the *Title* track. This opens the Video *Toolbox*. Click on the chapter buttons in the *Toolbox* window and they will highlight, even though they aren't linked to any chapters as yet. Select a button in your menu. Then select a clip in the *Video* track. Click on the *Set Chapter* icon in the *Toolbox*. A small icon will appear in the *Menu* track to indicate the location of the chapter.

3 In our example, the main menu (colour-coded pink in the *Menu* track) links to two separate titles – the wedding video and the extras section of the disc. Both of these titles have their own chapter menus. Studio colour-codes the menus and associated chapters separately to give you a quick visual indication of which chapters are linked to which menus.

4 You can place menus anywhere in the *Timeline* and link them to their relevant chapters using the *Toolbox*. Here we see the main menu (M1), the Wedding menu (M2), and the Extras menu featuring outtakes and miscellaneous material (M3). Use the *Set Return* option in the Toolbox to make the DVD return to the relevant menu after a title has finished playing. You can easily relink your assets by dragging the flags around in the *Menu* track.

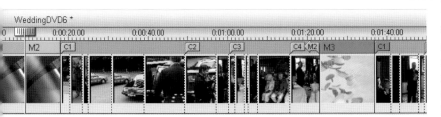

Finalizing the menu

Before you risk burning your DVD to disc, take it for a test drive

No matter how well organized you are in the planning stages, things can still go wrong during production. You may have a faulty link that goes to the wrong submenu, or you may have forgotten to create a 'next' or 'back' button. Spend some time checking your DVD to make sure that it delivers what you planned it to deliver – interesting content accessible by a well-designed menu. You can become so familiar with a DVD project that you begin to overlook errors.

Right: *Use the remote control to check that the DVD's navigation works before burning your DVD.*

This is why a proper proofing stage is so important. Even if you're only working on a compilation of family moments, producing a DVD that doesn't work can be annoying. Not only do you end up wasting time, but you end up wasting discs. If you're producing professional work – such as an electronic portfolio or video brochure – or something for more widespread consumption, then any mistakes will be more serious and more embarrassing.

Run through the disc yourself, checking that every button or link leads where it should and does what it says. Then get a friend who is unfamiliar with the project to test it out. They may uncover unforeseen navigation problems. Some applications are friendly enough to spot some problems themselves. In iDVD for example, should you forget to add slides to a slideshow, the

software will warn you that you have to have at least one slide in a slideshow when you click on the *Burn* icon. However, the program can never catch everything for you, so give your DVD a thorough 'test drive' before you burn.

Now is also the time to check your status pane (or equivalent) and make sure you haven't exceeded the storage capacity of a standard blank DVD-R disc. All your video, music, and stills, plus any other content you want to add, needs to weigh in at under 4.7GB (or 8.5GB if you use a dual-layer drive and your software supports it). Your PC or Mac also has to encode all of your project's assets to

make them playable on a DVD player. This means you'll have to make sure that your hard drive has at least twice as much free space available as your DVD project uses or you could run into trouble. If your project is 3GB, make sure you have 6GB free on your hard drive.

Once you're happy previewing the disc, click on the *Burn* icon. The amount of time the process will take is dependent on your computer's DVD burner. If you have lots of menu transitions, the disc will take longer to burn. While the laser is searing the content onto your DVD, go and make yourself a well-earned coffee.

Test drive

When you type an important document your computer package operates various tools to help you get it perfect – the spell checker and the grammar checker, for example. Entry-level DVD packages – and their more sophisticated cousins – allow you to test-drive the DVD before burning it to disc. They do this by giving you a remote control simulator. This virtual device appears on your PC's screen and allows you to navigate around your disc's content just as the end-user will do with their handheld remote. It is essential that you preview your disc using this simulator, so that you can find broken links and fix them before unleashing the disc on the public. A faulty disc will only cost you later.

Below: *The finished Hoover Dam Visit DVD in action. The buttons are now functional, as you can see from the highlight on the Scene Selection button.*

Add a Title Screen

When you load a professional DVD disc into your player, a copyright warning appears before the main menu. This Title Screen plays for a few seconds before the main menu appears. You can create your own Title Screen message to make the user feel that they are watching a professional disc – just design the copyright warning in Photoshop and add it to the project's hierarchy so that it is displayed before the main menu appears. You can also create a still or animated logo. iDVD's *Map* pane allows you to drag and drop stills and movies into the DVD menu hierarchy so that they appear before the main menu is displayed.

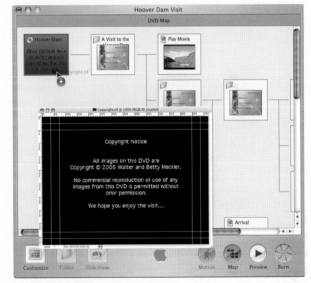

Above: *Make a logo movie or copyright image play before the main menu appears.*

Left: *Check that each option in the chapter selection menu takes you through to the correct part of the movie. Burning a faulty disc can be a source of frustration later on.*

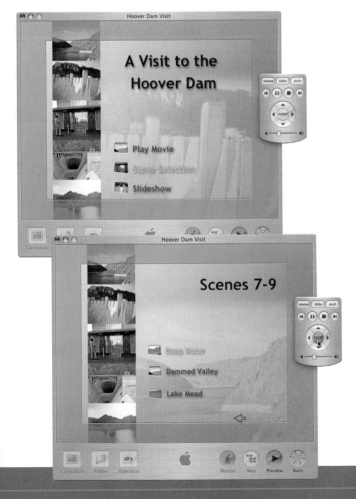

Creating more complex menus

You can't deny it – a template is a very handy springboard from which to get your DVD up and running in a short amount of time – and this is as true of prosumer-level applications as it is of the basic packages. Apple's DVD Studio Pro and Adobe Encore feature dozens of editable templates covering a variety of popular topics.

Even if you use rival packages, don't skip this section as the principles of menu design can be applied to any DVD authoring software. All DVD menus are limited to a maximum of 36 chapters, for example. Limitations like this mean that form follows function – your menu has to work within the constraints of the medium.

As discussed earlier in this chapter, Apple's domestic iDVD package gives you themed template designs that you can adapt. As you'd expect from a more sophisticated (and more expensive) package, Apple's DVD Studio Pro offers a greater variety of templates. Most of these templates come with a selection of submenu designs that are variations on the main theme. This enables you to have more variety in your menu design while at the same time maintaining a coherent look for the DVD as a whole.

Right: *The templates in DVD Studio Pro are more oriented towards the professional market than iDVD's themes. Weddings and corporate presentations are well catered for, along with some exciting, highly adaptable styles.*

Left: *As well as a cover page, many of the DVD Studio Pro templates come with compatibly designed submenu pages. As with iDVD, you can drag and drop components into the window of the template to begin customizing it.*

Left: *Templates are professionally designed to display your DVD's contents in innovative ways. You can adapt this cityscape style menu by adding stills or motion menus to the billboards.*

Customizing Studio Pro menus

Even if you're a professional, it makes sense to use templates. They take less time to create and less time to troubleshoot than a menu built from scratch. The advantage of using DVD Studio Pro or DVD Encore is that you can easily take the application's existing templates, then customize them to create a menu that looks unique.

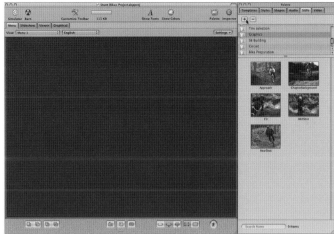

1 Create a new DVD Studio Pro project. Go to *Preferences* to choose the NTSC or PAL format and import your assets into the project. Go to the *Still* tab to import the screenshots and source images you need for your menu, then click *Add*. Do the same with the *Video* tab and import any movie components.

2 Go to the *Template* tab, and double-click on any of the pre-designed options to see what is available. The template, Leader Detail, has a movie playing in the background. Click on the *Motion* icon (the walking man) to watch a preview.

3 The first change to make is to replace the template's default background movie with one of your own video clips. Go to the *Video* tab and drag a movie clip onto the main window, dragging and dropping it over the existing background movie. Make sure you don't place it in a smaller window by mistake. You'll get a pop-up menu that allows you to assign commands. Select *Set Background*. Click on the *Motion* icon to watch the clip loop.

4 Drag the same video clip from the *Video* tab into the smaller window below the *Secondary Title* section. You could add a different clip or a still image here, but having two of the same clip playing alongside each other will link the foreground and background elements together, as the movement in one clip echoes the other.

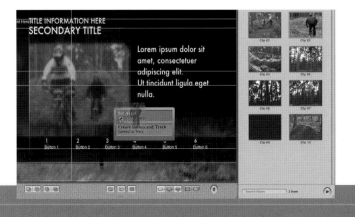

5 DVD Studio Pro comes with a variety of preset shapes you can use to augment a menu. The Leader template that we're adapting contains a gradient, found in the *Shapes* pane, that goes from black to transparent. The *Shapes* pane can be used to customize existing templates or to help create menus from scratch. You can select the gradient shape in the main menu and resize it by dragging the handles on the edge of the shape.

Guides
The yellow guides are a great help when you're trying to position elements on your menu, but a distraction when you're trying to get a feel for the finished result. To see the template menu shaping up as you customize it, go to *View* and select *Hide Guides*. You can always turn them on again later.

6 This template comes with default buttons. Delete the ones you don't need by selecting them and hitting backspace. Click on the remaining buttons and change their text to something more appropriate to your disc's content. The descriptions 'Button 1', 'Button 2', and so on, are labels to help you. They won't appear in the finished menu. Drag the buttons and automatic yellow guides will help you reposition each button and keep it aligned with the others.

7 Add images edited in Photoshop to help customize your DVD Studio Pro template. Drag these images from the *Stills* palette onto the main window. Find a clear space (don't place them in existing boxes) and select either *Create Button* or *Create Drop Zone* from the pop-up menu. You can use the *Drop Zone* option to add a variety of extra components to your menu within Studio Pro. Scale these elements and keep their proportions accurate by holding down the Shift key.

Alpha channels
As you can see from the circular icons in our example, DVD Studio Pro can read alpha channels created in Photoshop to make the edges of the image transparent. This means your imported graphics don't have to have a visible rectangular border.

8 Once your graphics and movies have been imported and positioned, your menu should bear little resemblance to the original template. Click on *Simulate* to see how it will look when played from a DVD disc.

Using Adobe Encore

Like its Mac equivalent Studio Pro, Adobe Encore contains pre-designed menu templates. However, as part of the Adobe family, Encore also appeals to designers who want to create their menus from scratch in Photoshop rather than adapt existing designs. Encore is designed to fit smoothly into an Adobe creative pipeline, using Premiere Pro to edit footage, and Photoshop to create source material for the menu, such as backgrounds, buttons, and subpictures. Encore's customizable interface and Photoshop layers compatibility help you fine-tune your design.

Being able to work across all the Adobe packages gives the designer greater control over the finished menu. You can assign chapter markers in Premiere Pro that will be read by Encore, or use Encore itself to assign chapter markers to edited footage. This freedom to jump back and forth between different packages helps you streamline your workflow, and is a major benefit for those who adopt the Adobe route.

An overview of the Adobe Encore 1.5 interface

The toolbox allows you to manipulate entire buttons using the Selection tool (the top arrow), or edit layered button components using the Direct Selection tool (the outlined arrow).

The Properties palette allows you to create motion menus by adding a video background, or creating animated buttons.

Encore is relatively intuitive and, like Photoshop, features a variety of ways to achieve the same result. Drag and drop a button element from the Library to add it to the menu. Right-clicking the mouse brings up a handy context menu.

As with Photoshop, Encore's tabbed floating windows can be docked together in a way that suits the user. This helps save valuable workspace.

The Layers palette shows you the various menu elements, from subpictures to backgrounds. All of this information can be read and edited in Photoshop, which is one of Encore's strengths.

The Library contains many sets of pre-designed menus and buttons, including the obligatory wedding templates and some corporate-themed assets.

Creating menus with Encore

1 Let's use Encore to create a variation on our extreme biking menu. In the *Library* palette, you can rummage through a variety of menu sets to find a suitable theme. We picked the Astroturf submenu from the Sports set and clicked on the *New Menu* icon at the bottom of the palette.

2 We'll need to import our own assets to customize the template. Go to the *Properties* palette. Right-click and choose the *Import as Asset* option to bring in your source stills and movies. Alternatively, drag and drop the images and movies into the Properties palette from Windows Explorer. If you bring in an AVI or QuickTime movie, Encore 1.5 will automatically transcode it into a DVD compatible MPEG-2 file. We imported our edited extreme cycling video, a montage of stunt highlights, and a few crash outtakes.

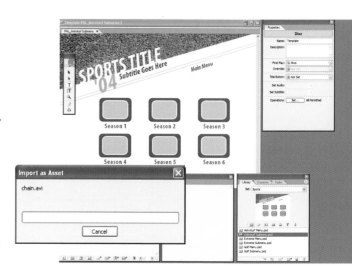

3 We decided to remove the buttons that came with the template and to create some more dynamic ones to suit our cycling DVD's subject matter. To lose unwanted buttons (or other menu elements), simply select them with the *Selection* tool and hit delete. We went to the *Library* and chose a slanted button from the Corporate set to give the menu's button a sense of dynamic movement. Right-clicking on this button allowed us to make it the default button. When any video elements are dragged to the main menu, they appear in that button automatically.

Edit in Photoshop
You can take any of the images from the template menu into Photoshop for further editing. Just right-click on them to get the pop-up context menu and select *Edit in Photoshop*. Alternatively, select the image and use the keyboard shortcut Shift + Control + M.

4 When you drag a clip to the main menu, it appears in the default button. You'll see from the *Properties* box that Encore usefully adds a link to make the button play the relevant clip and return the DVD to the main menu when the clip has finished playing. Label the button in the *Properties* palette so you can keep track of it in the *Layers* palette later. Use the *Selection* tool to resize the buttons (holding down Shift to constrain their proportions). We scaled the buttons to make them shrink from left to right, to create a sense of depth and perspective. The most important link – the main movie – appears largest and on the far left.

5 The default buttons we have created contain their own text field. To edit the text, select the *Direct Selection* tool and double-click on the button in the main menu window. Type in something more appropriate than the default word 'text'. Adjust the font, size, and colour of the text by clicking on the *Character* palette tab. The other text that comes with the main template menu can be edited using the same technique.

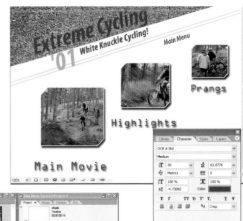

6 When we added the clips, a button with associated links was automatically created. Look in the *Properties* palette. You'll see that Encore has created a timeline for each button, which looks similar to the Premiere *Timeline*. Using it, extra audio tracks and subtitles can be added, as well as chapter markers if required. You can also move backwards and forwards through the *Timeline* and preview the content of the movie in the monitor window.

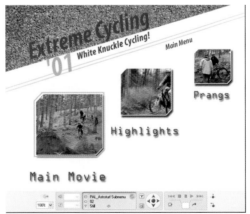

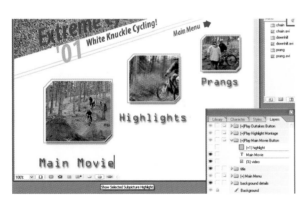

7 The template button we used from the *Library* has its own subpictures already added. At the bottom of the main menu is a selection of icons. You can click on these to see the subpicture highlights for the menu's various button states (like 'selected' or 'activated'). You can also see these highlights in the *Layers* palette, as each button has a folder containing its own graphic and subpicture components. These can be edited in Photoshop if required.

8 Creating a menu by adapting existing palettes is a fairly straightforward and quick process. Testing the menu to see how the DVD will behave is equally easy. Hit Control + Alt + the Space Bar to get a preview window. As with Studio Pro, iDVD, and Pinnacle Studio, you can simulate the behavior of your DVD menu before burning it to disc. It's especially useful to see how the subpictures behave and to check that the menu's components are correctly linked together.

Animated thumbnails

We created our buttons by dragging movie clips onto the menu. To animate them, select the main menu in the *Project* window, then go to the *Properties* palette. There's a handy *Animate Buttons* option, but you won't be able to preview the buttons moving until you go to *File > Render Motion*.

How interaction works on DVD

Link your menu elements together in a coherent and convenient way

As a DVD designer, it's easy to get bogged down in the interface aesthetics and forget that, ultimately, a menu's prime purpose is to serve the user. When you go to a restaurant, you want the menu to be easy to read so that it's easy to find your favourite dishes. You expect it to open with the starters, move on to the main courses, and finish with the dessert options.

A DVD menu exists to serve. To make the interaction between user and DVD menu as smooth as possible, you need to make it intuitive. For example, when the user is watching one deleted scene from a long list of options, they should return to the deleted scene menu to find that the next scene is automatically selected. By linking the end of one piece of video with the next scene icon in the list of menu items, you are saving the user hassle. Little touches like this help to give your DVD a professional feel.

DVD structure

In structural terms, the process of interacting with a DVD menu is similar to browsing the contents of a website. A DVD's main menu is the equivalent of a website's home page: it gives you a flavour of the disc's content, and access to a variety of submenus containing links to other submenus and back to the main menu.

Of course, the analogy breaks down when you look at the technology involved, but DVD remains a highly interactive medium. We already take for granted that a DVD user can access any point of a movie within seconds by jumping to pre-defined chapter markers. They can also access subtitles, separate audio commentaries, and parallel video tracks, or even watch alternative cuts of the movie.

All this interaction is made possible through the use of Program Chains (PGCs). To understand them, you need to understand that the video and audio data on a DVD is divided into cells, and a PGC

Right: *A simple example of what is known as "conditional branching" is when the DVD menu selects the next link in a list after playing a clip.*

effectively controls how those cells are linked together. When you play a simple movie from start to finish, the PGC strings the cells in order, from the first to the last. However, the PGC can do a lot more than that. It can control what video, audio, and subtitle files are played at any time, and also define how the user can navigate from one point to another on the disc.

While relatively primitive, PGC language can facilitate some quite sophisticated interactions, including conditional branching. A simple example of this is when the DVD menu takes the decision of what to offer the user next, based on where the user has just come from. At the most complex, this interaction can extend to the DVD making a decision about what version of a scene to show next, based on what version of a movie – theatrical or special edition – the user has elected to watch.

DVD and books

DVD interaction has much in common with the process of reading a book. A book has a title, and a DVD has a Video Title Set. Like books, DVD title sets are broken down into separate scenes called "Chapters." There is even a contents list printed inside the DVD's cover inlay that gives you clues about the content of each chapter. Some DVD players allow the viewer to place a virtual bookmark that ties in with the timecode on the disc so that, at some later time, they can jump to exactly where they left off.

Above: *The mouse is mightier than the remote. Unfortunately, most people will have to navigate around your disc using the limited arrow options of their hand-held remote.*

Controlling the DVD

DVD gives the viewer an awful lot of options, and while your authoring software will take care of the tricky PGC stuff for you, you still need to give thought to how all these options should connect, and how your DVD presents them. The biggest challenge when designing DVD menus is the method of control – the remote control. To return to the Web analogy, a surfer moves his or her mouse freely to point the cursor at a link on the page before clicking the mouse to access content on another page. Easy access all the way. The domestic DVD user interacts with the disc using a handheld remote control, which means they are forced to navigate using the remote's four arrows (to move up, down, left, or right).

It's crucial that you take this into account when designing your interface. As the user of a DVD menu will have to jump horizontally or vertically from one button to the next, it makes sense to lay the buttons out in vertical columns, horizontal rows, or grids – even if the design appears to be less rigid on the surface. The user can then see intuitively that to get from A to D, they will need to jump horizontally or vertically via buttons B and C. If the user has to stop and think about which button on their remote they need to press to get to the right button on the screen, your menu is not a success.

Simulator

menu | title

enter

01
03
02
✓ View

00:00:15

Ramps

Slalom

Big Air

Rollovers versus subpictures

DVD places other constraints on the menu designer other than the need to be navigable by remote control. Both Web and DVD designers have to create a way for the user to know that they have selected and activated an onscreen button. Web designers have the advantage here, thanks to rollover graphics. They can create a multi-coloured rollover graphic that changes state to show that a button has been selected. They could have a button that consists of a photograph of a closed human eye, for example. Moving the mouse over the eye would trigger the button to display a similar photo of an open eye, so creating an animated effect. What's more, depending on the technology used, each component of the rollover could be a full-colour photo or illustration, enabling some quite spectacular effects.

While the DVD designer can create the equivalent of a rollover to indicate the status of a button, the options as far as graphics are concerned are far more limited. Unlike its Web counterpart, the DVD graphic (subpicture) cannot be a full-colour photograph or illustration. A subpicture is limited to one colour – yellow is the most common – along with a level of transparency so that the multi-coloured background graphic

Above: *A subpicture is the DVD menu's version of a Web rollover. Notice the limited colour options. But a subpicture can be any shape.*

can still be seen underneath. The only additional option is to assign another colour to the subpicture to indicate that the user has pressed Return or Enter.

In other words, a DVD button has three states. The first state, Normal, is the button, unselected, and just an icon or text line that stands out of the menu's background image. The second state is Selected, with a colour-coded subpicture overlaid above the original graphic. The third state is Activated: the subpicture can change colour again to indicate that the user has pressed the Return button on their remote. When you compare it to animated Web buttons, this all seems distinctly unexciting for the DVD user. But don't worry, there are other ways to make your menu more of an experience.

Above: *The three states of the subpicture button: Normal, Selected, and Activated.*

Unlike its Web counterpart, the DVD subpicture cannot consist of a full-colour photograph or illustration.

Right: *A DVD menu is more than a series of clips linked by buttons. Animated chapter previews are one way of assisting the user's interaction.*

Creating rollover subpictures

When you design a menu using an existing template, the template will usually contain preset buttons, with subpictures assigned so that the user can select a button and see it highlighted, then press return and see another colour to indicate that the option has been activated. To do the same when you create your own menu from scratch, you need to design a subpicture rollover in a separate graphics application.

We're going to use Photoshop to create subpictures that suit the style of our DVD on extreme cycling. We can avoid the conventional rollover effect, whereby a coloured semi-transparent box appears over the scene preview window, and creates iconic subpicture shapes. We can then use an existing menu design as a guide to position our subpictures on a separate layer, then import them into DVD Studio Pro. The various colour states that indicate the status of the selected scene can still be applied to these shapes.

Guides

When laying out subpictures and menu items, it's useful to have guidelines. In Photoshop, press Command + R to activate the rulers. Then drag horizontal and vertical guides from the rulers onto the main image. Press Command + ; to hide the guides.

Right: *The colour state of the subpicture gives the user a source of visual feedback on the selection of items in the menu.*

1 Here's our Photoshop-designed menu for a page of scenes linking to various bike-related stunts and activities. The stills displaying various scenes are placeholder graphics. We'll add movie previews to those sections in our DVD application. Before creating a subpicture, give the placeholders a raised 3D look to enhance the design. Go to the *Blending Options* short-cut at the bottom of the *Layers* palette and choose *Bevel and Emboss* to open the *Layer Styles* window.

2 To edit the 3D look of the *Bevel*, click on the words *Bevel and Emboss* in the *Layer Styles* window. Set the *Style* to *Emboss* and the technique to *Chisel Hard*. Experiment with the *Depth* slider to get the type of 3D effect that you require. Set the *Direction* to *Up*. In the *Shading* section of the *Layer Styles* window you can change the direction of the light source to alter the highlights on the scene preview's edge. This helps the preview stand out from the background.

3 Once you're happy with the 3D Bevel, you can apply the same layer style to the other scene preview graphics. You don't need to edit each layer separately. Simply go to the *Layers* palette and drag the new *Effects* icon from under the first layer and place it below a layer containing a different graphic. Any effect you have added to one layer will then automatically be applied to the other layer, giving a consistent look to all of your elements.

4 Use the *Type* tool (T) to add text to various layers. Experiment with fonts that suit your menu interface. In our example, we chose the Ocra font to tie it in with the number on the bike in the menu background. Use the *Move* tool (V) to position the text next to the scene preview windows. Use *Layer Styles* to add a *Drop Shadow* effect to the text. In a few steps, we'll create a subpicture layer using the text we've created.

5 A DVD menu would be incomplete without navigation symbols to link to the next set of chapters and back to the main menu. These symbols also need subpictures. To create the icons, go to the *Custom Shape* tool in the toolbar. From the *Shape* options bar, choose *Arrows*. Select a shape and draw with the *Custom Shape* tool (U) to add the icon to the menu. Use the *Free Transform* tool (Command + T) to scale and rotate the icons if required.

6 Use the *Custom Shape* tool to create an additional subpicture graphic that will only appear when the user selects a chapter window. You could draw this subpicture icon using the *Pen* tool (P). Clicking with the *Pen* tool creates filled vector shapes. You can fine-tune these shapes by using the *Direct Selection* tool, which repositions the anchor points that you placed with the *Pen* tool. Alternatively, grab another vector symbol from the *Custom Shape* picker.

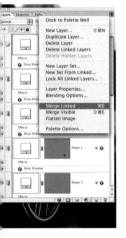

7 Once you've finished designing your subpicture graphics, they need to be turned into a flattened layer that will be used by DVD Studio Pro to create interactive subpictures that appear when a chapter preview is selected. Select the text and icon layers and click the chain icons next to the layer thumbnails to link them together. From the *Layers* palette choose *Merged Linked* to flatten the icon layers together.

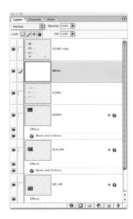

8 To duplicate this flattened icon layer, go to the main menu and choose *Image*, then *Invert*. This will turn the white text and icons to black. Create a new layer in the *Layers* palette and fill it with white. Link the black-and-white layers together. Select the new layer, copy it, and paste it into its own file. Save this file as a TIFF. DVD Studio Pro will use this black-and-white TIFF to create the colour rollovers that appear over the DVD menu.

Creating rollover effects for Adobe Encore

PC users with access to Adobe Encore have an advantage over Mac users when it comes to subpicture creation. As we've just seen, Mac users need to create a black-and-white subpicture layer to overlay on their menu in DVD Studio Pro, and then add colour to these subpictures in DVD Studio Pro. When using Encore, the DVD designer can create a layered Photoshop file that contains buttons, backgrounds, and subpictures, then export the layered file straight into Encore. In addition, the PC user can then send files from Encore to After Effects to create motion menus. This interactivity between the main Adobe products streamlines the DVD design workflow – and while working with Photoshop has improved vastly in DVD Studio Pro 3, it's still an advantage that non-Encore users should envy.

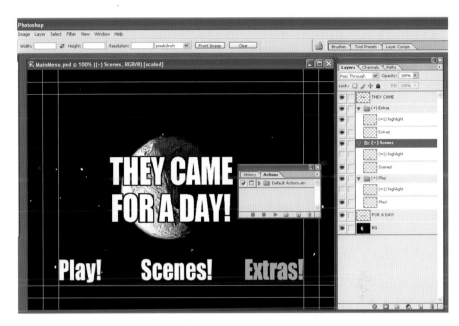

Top right: *PC users can design their subpicture rollover graphics in Photoshop and import the layered files straight into Adobe Encore.*

Right: *Unlike DVD Studio Pro, Encore reads all the layers from Photoshop, allowing you greater creative control over your menu authoring once it's been designed. Encore can also read the colour and opacity values of subpicture layers, which saves you having to colour map as you do in Studio Pro.*

Importing rollover subpictures into DVD Studio Pro

The DVD Studio Pro interface can feel overpowering when you first see it. You have the option to use a basic version of the interface, but to add subpictures and apply colours to indicate the various states the buttons are in, we'll need to use the advanced version. This is your opportunity to familiarize yourself with the main elements of Studio Pro and how they perform when adding and creating subpicture rollovers.

Separate states

The Normal state of our unselected button is white, which is the colour we set the button graphics in Photoshop. We can use Color Mapping to assign other colours to the black-and-white subpicture layer to indicate other button states.

The DVD Studio Pro advanced interface

The Inspector *gives you editable information about whatever asset you have selected. In this example, we change the colour of the button rollover states.*

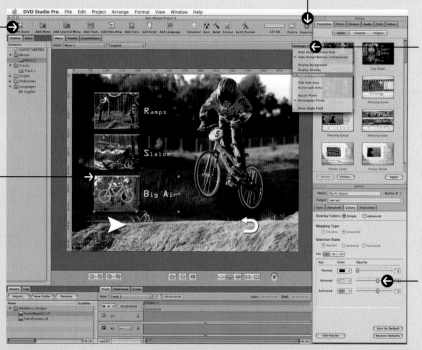

Import any stills or video clips into the Assets tab. You can drag them from here onto the main menu window.

Create a button by drawing a rectangle over the background graphic and the hidden subpicture layer. Even though we only have two layered stills in this project, we can create many buttons from them.

The Settings option lets you view your graphics and subpictures either separately or as a composite.

These icons are important in relation to rollovers. They display the different states of your buttons and show you the colours you've assigned to each state. From left to right, they show you a button's Normal state, its Selected state, and its Activated state. In this example, the button's Selected state is yellow.

Importing rollover subpictures into DVD Studio Pro

Assigning colours and Opacity settings to rollover graphics to indicate
the different states of the buttons

1 Start by opening Studio Pro. Go to *File → New* to
create a new project. Go to the *Assets* tab and click on
Import. Select the folder containing the background
scene menu image and the subpicture Tiff file you
created in Photoshop (*see pages 54-56*). Once the files
are imported, drag the background image into the
menu design window. Choose *Set Background* from the
pop-up window.

2 Drag the black-and-white subpictures image from
the *Assets* tab onto the main window. Choose
Create Overlay from the pop-up window. You won't
see anything happen, which can be confusing.
Don't worry. If you look at the *Inspector*, you'll see
that the file you imported has been set to *Overlay*.
You'll be able to see the effect of this overlay once
you assign buttons to the main menu.

3 Go to the *Settings* option and
set it to *Display Composite*.
This will let you see the
subpictures once you've
assigned a button to them
and chosen a colour to
represent the different button
states. Draw a rectangular
button over one of the
chapter selection windows.
Make sure the rectangle is
large enough to cover the
relevant parts of the hidden
subpicture layer.

4 This rectangular button selection will
cause the appropriate part of the
hidden subpicture overlay to appear
when the DVD user selects it. Once
you've drawn a button, go to the
Inspector and choose the *Color
Settings* tab. Go to the *Selected*
section and choose a colour for the
subpicture to indicate that the user
has selected this menu button.
Choose a different colour for the
Activated state. Set the *Opacity* to
9 so the user can see through the
subpicture when it is selected.

Using subpictures
Linking subpictures to video

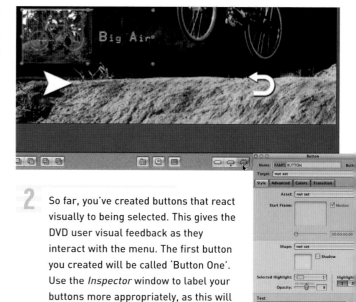

Having transferred our subpictures from Photoshop to Studio Pro, we need to connect everything up so it works. But it's worth testing the menu first to make sure it is fully functional.

1 To test different button subpicture states, make sure that you've checked the *Display Composite* option in the *Settings* section so that you can see the different states superimposed on the background graphic. Just beneath the main menu window are three state icons. In this example, we've selected the icon that displays a button's *Activated* state. Test each state of your menu buttons to make sure they are displaying the correct colours.

2 So far, you've created buttons that react visually to being selected. This gives the DVD user visual feedback as they interact with the menu. The first button you created will be called 'Button One'. Use the *Inspector* window to label your buttons more appropriately, as this will help you organize the project as it becomes more complex. Once you've created different states for the button subpictures, you need to link each to a movie clip.

3 To give the buttons a video clip to link to, import some movie assets into the project. Go to the *Video* tab in the *Palette* window and click on the + icon. Navigate to the relevant movie file on your hard drive and click *Add* to import it into the project. To add the imported video track to the DVD menu, drag it from the *Palette* onto the V1 track of the *Track Editor*. Notice that any iMovie-assigned chapter markers will automatically appear in the *Timeline*.

4 To link a button to its appropriate chapter, right-click (or Control-click if you're using a one-button mouse) on the button and select *Target* from the pop-up menu. Go to *Tracks and Stories* and choose the relevant chapter name from the *Track* option. This technique is similar to the way you link HTML files together using Web authoring packages.

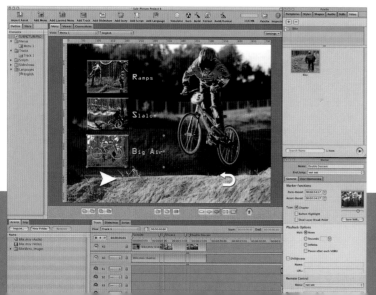

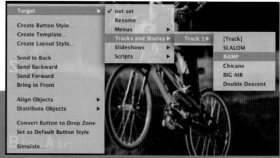

5 As this chapter menu is the first menu that's been added to the project, it is automatically labeled Menu 1. We can use the *Inspector* window to change the name to 'Chapter Menu'. The project will make more sense as it develops if we label things accurately now.

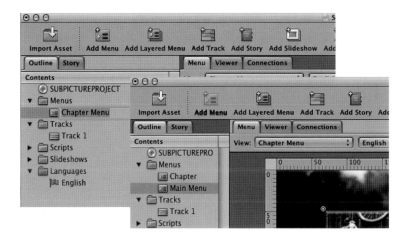

6 The Chapter Menu won't be the first menu the user sees on activating the DVD. You need to create a main menu that links to the Chapter Menu and other submenus. Import a new background and any subpicture assets for the main menu using the techniques covered on page 45. Then go to the icon bar at the top of the screen and click the *Add Menu* icon. This adds a new blank menu to the project. Label it 'Main Menu'.

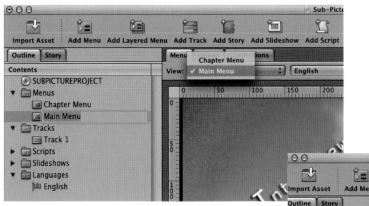

7 Select the new menu using the *Menu* tab's *View* option. You can then add the relevant graphics and subpictures to the new Main Menu and create an interactive button that links to the Chapter Menu (see the previous two pages for details, choosing *Target →* *Menus* to select the appropriate menu). Make sure that you also create a button from the Chapter Menu that will take you back to the Main Menu. Slowly but surely, your DVD is becoming more interactive.

8 In our example, the main movie has been placed in the *Timeline* on Track 1. When the movie has finished playing, you'll need to tell the DVD player to return automatically to the Main Menu (or a submenu). Select the track in the *Outline* tab at the top-left of the interface. Then go to the *Inspector* window and use the *End Jump* option to tell the DVD to jump to the Main Menu after the movie finishes playing.

Showcase

Creature Comforts

The designers of the *Creature Comforts* DVD explain their approach to menu design.

'Basically, we had to pitch the concept of having a machine as the main interface. They went for it.'

Creature Comforts is a series of short stop-motion animations featuring a variety of animals being interviewed on camera. The creatures are voiced by members of the public, who were recorded on tape. Aardman, the company behind the comedy duo Wallace and Gromit, created a variety of model animals to fit the voices and personalities of the interviewees.

We talked to the designer Tim Long from design company DGP about his design work on the menu for the *Creature Comforts* DVD.

Aardman's animated output tends to feature distinctive looking stop-motion characters interacting with crazy retro-style gadgets, like the radio-controlled techno-trousers in the Oscar-winning short film *The Wrong Trousers*.

When designing the menu for *Creature Comforts*, Tim was keen to capture this trademark visual style. The machines in Aardman's animations tend to be overly complex for their simple functions, and have an old-fashioned appearance, characterized by valves, dials, and levers. The final menu features an appropriately retro machine, with various buttons surrounding a screen to access the content. Tim worked closely with Aardman to create a suitable design.

'Basically, we had to pitch the concept of having a machine as the main interface. They went for it. I then said this was going to go work much better if they could build the model for us. They agreed to get their set builders to build this little contraption.'

As well as building the machine that forms the DVD's main interface, Aardman had to animate it in the style of the animations on the disc. Once Tim had a series of animations featuring the machine in action, he was ready to make it an interactive part of the DVD menu.

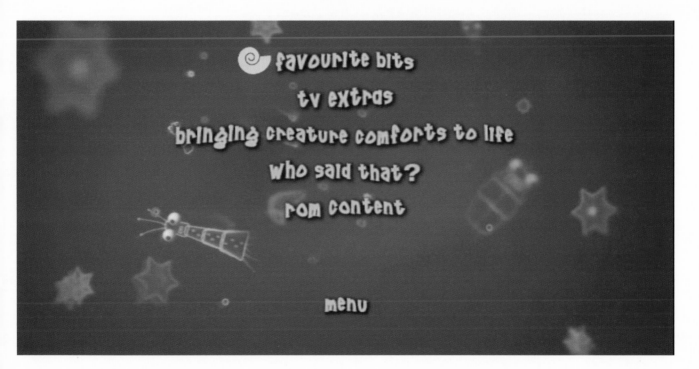

Opposite page: *Oscar-winning animation company Aardman created an old-fashioned looking machine to form the main component of the Creature Comforts DVD menu.*

Above: *The bonus menu echoes the creature-themed content of the DVD with the animated plankton floating in the background. A filter was added to the menu's background movie to make it ripple as if underwater.*

Left: *When the Creature Comforts DVD's main menu appears, it shows a looping movie featuring the machine Aardman designed and animated especially for the DVD. Lights flash, levers move back and forth, and old-fashioned reel-to-reel tapes rotate. Video clips from the disc's various episodes play in a monitor at the centre of the machine. The clips have video filters added to them to make them appear scratchy and distorted. This reflects the eccentric nature of the machines in the Aardman universe. The impression is that the contraption could go haywire and break down at any moment.*

As the user makes a menu selection with their DVD's remote, coloured subpictures are overlaid on the various buttons in the main menu.

Right: The Creature Comforts *menu, like many menus, features animated transitions. These short clips play when a menu choice has been made, taking the viewer from the main menu to a submenu, for example. In this case, the transition movie shows as static appearing on the screen, which settles down to reveal the episode choices. Transitions can be tricky to do well. If the menu is animating on a loop, there is little the designer can do to make the transition a seamless one, as you can't predict the moment at which the DVD user will press a button. There will invariably be a jump from the main menu movie to the transition movie.*

To minimize this jump, DGP designer Kathryn Davey has some tips:

'The first frame of the transition should be as generic as possible so that not a lot seems to move from one frame to the other. Another option is to hide the transition by adding a white flash, a sudden movement, or even a distracting sound effect.'

Right: *Another technical constraint faced by DVD designers is the phenomenon of sound clipping, especially on a transition movie. All DVD players are different, and some are faster than others at playing a transition. On the slower machines, the first few frames of sound in a transition movie may be cut short, which stops the transition from appearing seamless.*

Tim gave us some tips on avoiding unprofessional sound clips: 'We leave eight frames clear of sound at the start of the transition. You can have eight frames of movement, but DVD players tend to clip the audio, so if you're going for a big, distracting transition, coming in with a bang or a whoosh, make the sound fade in eight frames after the transition begins or the bang or the whoosh is going to get clipped and it will be noticed.'

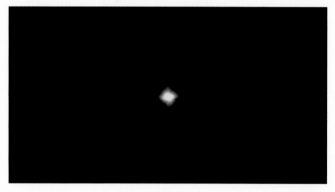

'In animation, half the effect is the sound'

Above: *The animation in the* Creature Comforts *menu is made all the more impressive by an appropriate use of sound. Tim chose his sound effects with care to ensure that they complemented the animation. Sound effects of cranking levers and whirring reels all added depth and believability to the menu, as Tim explains: 'In animation, half the effect is the sound. We went through all our sound sources and picked out loads of Aardman-esque sounds, then sent them down to Aardman for approval. With appropriate sound effects, a menu can stay relatively simple visually, but seem more complex and sophisticated.' Once an episode has been selected, the reels whirr and the video clips on the machine's monitor start to fast-forward. We exit the main menu with the screen turning black via a shrinking white dot. The transition fits perfectly with the low-tech style of the menu.*

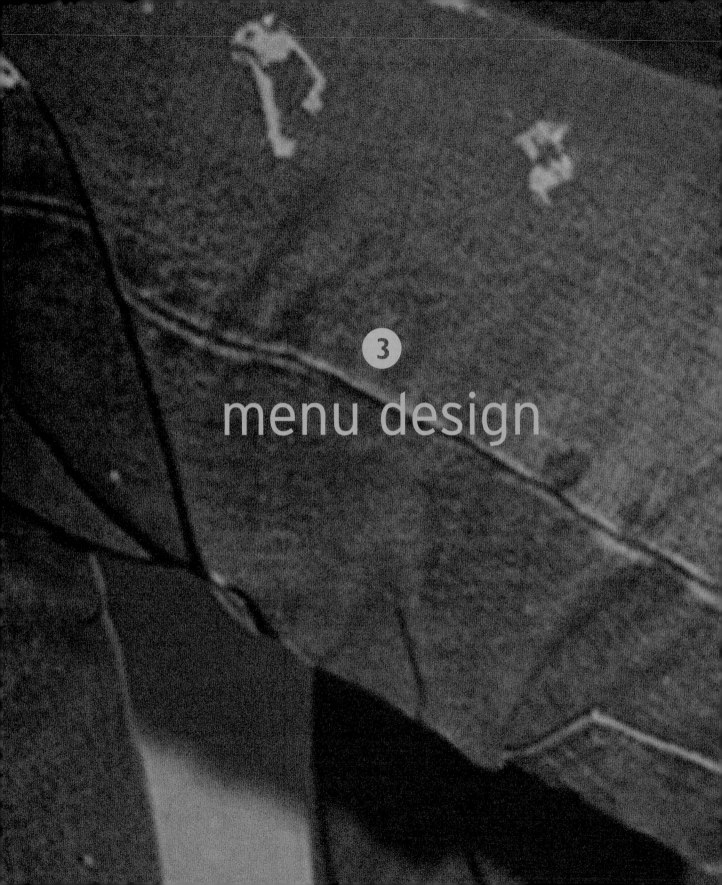

3

menu design

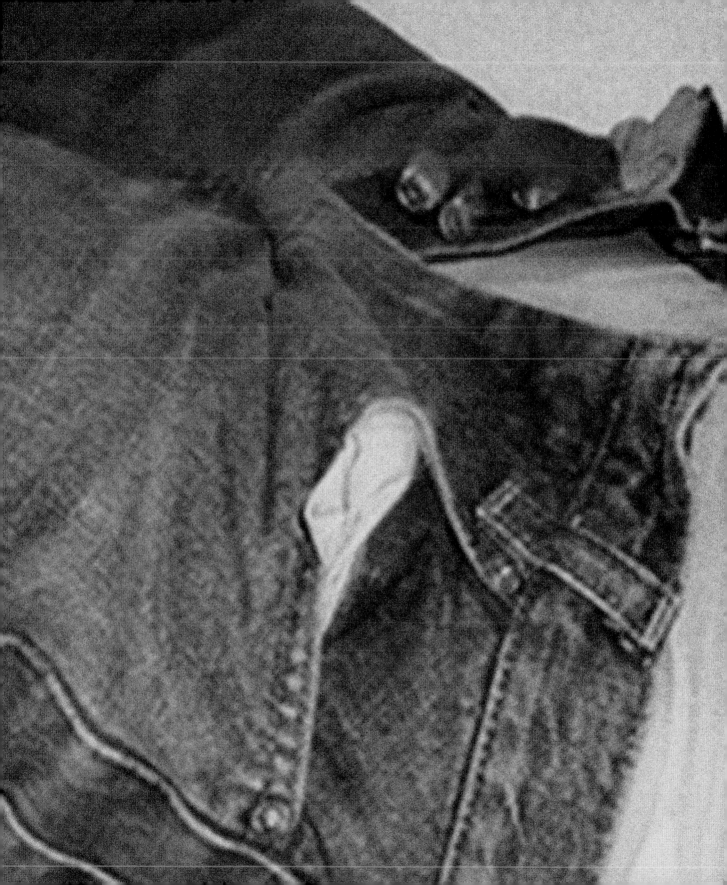

Overview of DVD menu design

The art of creating compelling DVD menus relies less on the strength of your DVD authoring application than on your skill with image editing, motion graphics, and 3D modeling applications. In a professional DVD production environment, the process involves more than one person. Often a designer and a DVD author work together, with the designer planning the screens and assigning subpictures for the DVD author to work with. But even when working on your own, there are rules and conventions to follow.

Below: *Applications such as Apple's iDVD provide a whole host of menu templates, ready for you to customize by adding content. Use the templates for inspiration or to try out ideas.*

Content

The way you design a DVD menu depends on what type of DVD it is. You can create a simple menu for a corporate presentation, but take the same content and present it as part of a design portfolio, complete with composited layers, animations, and accompanying audio effects. Unless you have included a 'first play' sequence, your menu is the first thing that the viewer sees when they play the DVD. As such, it should establish the characteristics of the content that follows and brand it with an identity all of its own.

So the first thing to consider is the content itself. What is going on the disc, who is going to view it, and is it likely to be played on a computer or DVD player? These are all factors to consider before you draw up any designs. Think about your audience – should the content be upfront and

quick to access or can you have fun with navigation? Should the interface consist of moving or still menus, with transitions or without, audio or silent, and so on. Some decisions will be entirely down to what you want or what the client wants.

You also need to know exactly what content you will have at your disposal, so that you can then organize a working structure for the disc accordingly. For all these processes, a rough storyboard can be very helpful.

saalbach 04
footage
gallery
audio

Title Safe
Action Safe

Left: *This is a shot of the main menu screen of a DVD of home movies. Designed according to professional standards, it has all the main interface elements within what is termed the 'title safe' area, while all the significant detail of the background image lies within the outer, 'action safe' rectangle.*

Establish a theme

Design your menu based on the content, following its themes, to establish the mood for what is to come. This may involve referencing the material on your disc and deriving the elements of your menu from the disc itself – this model is widely used in professional DVD menus for Hollywood movies. It provides a consistent and easy way to link between the menu and content.

If you don't have any visual material to work with or you are trying to show off your design skills, you could base your menu on a concept inspired by, but not referencing, the content. Be warned, however, that you could just as easily lose your audience as dazzle them with your talent, so make sure your menu has some relevance, no matter how abstract. Most consumer-level DVD authoring applications offer some templates on generic concepts – sun, sea, and sand elements for holidays, or rings and flower bouquets for weddings, for

example. These are included for a reason, being tried and tested design ideas, so even if you want to avoid cliché, don't be too proud to draw on them for inspiration.

The menu system

Your menu is merely an interface by which the user can access content in a logical and interactive manner. Although you can steer the user through the disc, you'll want to give them the most freedom to explore and enjoy the material as possible. The menu system relies on the use of buttons, but these can take any form you wish. They can look like the VCR controls of old, can be simple text links, or can resemble something far more surreal. It's entirely up to you, but remember – your aim is to ensure navigation to the content, so designing a clever link that doesn't appear to be a button is counterproductive. It's also important to give the user feedback that the button

they pressed has actually had an effect. This can be carried out by a change in colour or a highlight over the button, making use of a subpicture overlay.

You may also want to go down the Hollywood route of inserting short motion transitions between menus and content. This lets the user know the button click has had the desired effect, but is not suitable for all genres of DVD and is likely to pale with repeated use.

As well as a play button and any extra options, it's good practice to create and assign buttons for audio and subtitle tracks on the main page. These are important elements in the menu system, so access should be made available at the highest level.

Design rules

Designing for television is far more rule governed than designing for the Web, or multimedia design on a computer screen – there are all sorts of factors to take into account. To ensure that your DVD will operate on TV, you have to be aware of screen aspect ratios, as well as TV-safe colours and resolutions for the different TV systems. You'll need to plan your menu and storyboard how each menu connects to others.

When designing in Photoshop or another image editor, the background image should fill the entire document, but text and buttons should be kept within the safe area. These safety zones are known as the 'action safe' and 'title safe' areas and are shown on screen as

a pair of concentric rectangles. As a designer, you need to take into account broadcast safe areas for text and background elements, or you'll find that your menu is truncated and of little practical use. No text or options that are part of your menu should be outside title safe and nothing that you want to appear on your menu should be outside action safe (the outer rectangle). Adobe Photoshop CS provides preset file sizes in the Preset menu of the *New File* command that lets you create a document with nonprinting guides that delineate the action safe and title safe areas of the image. Note that this is only a problem on television due to the distortion caused by TV overscan – on PC monitors, your viewers will get to see the whole screen.

Another concern when designing for TV screens is the aspect ratio: the screen format of the TV in terms of the ratio of width to height. Is it to be 16:9 – the standard ratio for 'widescreen' sets – or the traditional 4:3 ratio? You need to know the aspect ratio in order to avoid your menu being distorted when on a TV screen. Unlike computer monitors, TV screens display non-square images, but image-authoring applications such as Photoshop CS allow you to create and

Left: *These shock tactics won't get you anywhere in menu design. While the ugly clash of colours is sure to capture the viewer's attention, the bright reds and greens stretch beyond the broadcast-safe palette of colours, and will look even worse on some TV screens than they do here.*

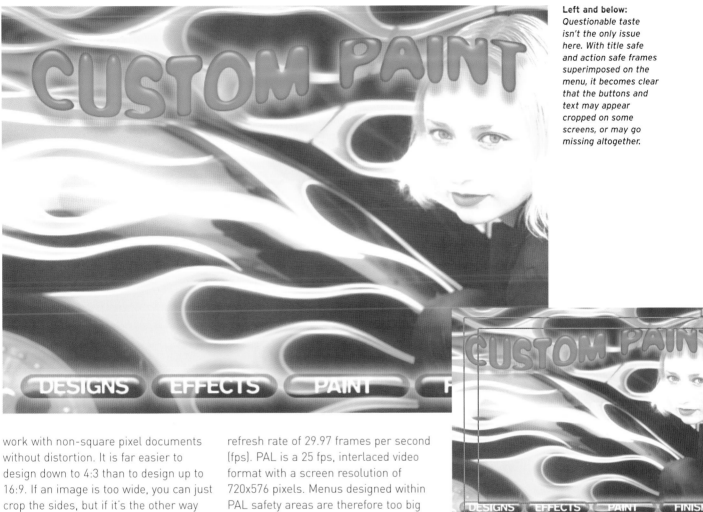

Left and below:
Questionable taste isn't the only issue here. With title safe and action safe frames superimposed on the menu, it becomes clear that the buttons and text may appear cropped on some screens, or may go missing altogether.

work with non-square pixel documents without distortion. It is far easier to design down to 4:3 than to design up to 16:9. If an image is too wide, you can just crop the sides, but if it's the other way around, you have to extend the design.

You also need to know if the finished DVD will play on NTSC (which operates predominantly in the US and Japan) or PAL (mainly UK and Europe). Each video standard has its own resolution: NTSC is an interlaced format comprising approximately 720x480 pixels with a refresh rate of 29.97 frames per second (fps). PAL is a 25 fps, interlaced video format with a screen resolution of 720x576 pixels. Menus designed within PAL safety areas are therefore too big for NTSC, leading many professional designers to apply a NTSC safety grid to the menu by default. In the future you may also need to worry about another format: HDTV (high definition television). This is planned to supplant both existing formats in time, but is not widespread at the time of writing.

You have to be aware of screen aspect ratios, TV-safe colours, and resolutions for the different TV systems

General principles of menu design

DVDs are used to deliver a variety of content and are intended for a diverse range of audiences. However, they all need a well-designed menu through which to control and access that content. General guidelines exist for creating any graphical user interface, of which a DVD menu is a prime example. Let's take a look at some of these guidelines in greater detail, so that we can begin to build some best practice principles for DVD menu design.

Layout

Pay particular attention to the layout of your menu, or 'composition' as it's known in design terms. Provide a focal point to the menu or you'll lose your audience. Don't add too many focal points. A collection of disparate graphics and text will only clutter up your menu unless they serve a purpose.

Left: *Using directional text and graphics will lead the viewer's eye to the main options on the menu.*

Above and left: *Bold graphics give a menu a dynamic feel, and are ideal for reworking as animated transitions later.*

Right: *Empty space is just as important as text or graphics, as it keeps the other elements in balance.*

You should always aim to make your menu appear slick and professional, and extraneous elements only serve to detract from the usability of the interface. Designers use directional text and graphics to ensure that the viewer follows a path to the important parts of an image. You can do this by giving the text an angle or making use of images in such a way that the eye is led across the screen. This also lends a sense of dynamism to even the most static background.

Empty space is as much a part of a menu design as stylized text or graphics. If used correctly, it can serve as a balance to your other elements and also as a way of highlighting the most important parts of your menu. Related elements can be grouped together to suggest a relationship and provide more of a visual impact; the tighter the group, the more important the relationship. On the other hand, space can be used to divide unrelated elements and so denote separate functions. DVD authoring packages have specific tools that do this for you, which are able to distribute objects and buttons evenly either horizontally or vertically.

Where you place elements of the composition, as well as the use of specific dominant colours or fonts, can indicate levels of importance in the menu. Think things through carefully and you'll be able to guide your viewer to the most important elements with ease. Alignment and symmetry of elements is important, giving a sense of balance to your composition. Most authoring packages allow you to align buttons and subpictures with the horizontal or vertical axes, or with the border of the title safe area.

Above all, be sure to repeat the basic format of your layout on every menu and submenu screen. Use the same type of background, the same iconography,

Radiohead: *7 Television Commercials*

This DVD collection of seven Radiohead videos was created at Abbey Road Interactive and features only one menu and intro, mainly because the team were only supplied with the packaging artwork.

Taking elements from the packaging, the designer changed their format and re-arranged them for a television screen. The type from the packaging and its background illustration were positioned in the middle, leaving the title to be placed in a left-hand vertical arrangement. This meant it did not overcrowd the central area.

The subpictures were rendered in the same scratchy style as the text, which helps to cover up the fact they are hard edged. The busy background also helps the subpictures blend in.

the same spacing and arrangements, similar colour combinations, and identical fonts and typefaces. This repetition will give a consistent, professional look to your production and makes for a user-friendly menu.

Text

We will be looking at fonts, backgrounds, and colours in more detail later in this chapter. For now, be aware that there are tried and tested design rules about text on screen. They include the use of contrasting colours for legibility, avoiding glaring colours or indistinct font sizes, and keeping any text conventions consistent across menus and submenus.

Menu options and buttons

No matter who your intended audience, it is important to keep the menu simple. Simple in this case doesn't necessarily mean simplistic, it means the interface should be uncluttered, uncomplicated, and easy to use. Not all of your viewers will have experience in navigating multimedia CD-ROMs or even webpages, so while you should avoid patronizing your viewer, you should never assume a level of understanding.

The most basic menu has options that link to the main content and perhaps a couple of basic selection buttons. Navigation buttons should be obvious in their function. If not, keep them clearly labelled. Even if they are custom-built, you can still keep to such conventions as back, forward, main menu, and play movie.

Button sizes need to be at least 70x60 pixels in order to show up on TV, so this limits the amount you can have on screen. Although you can have a maximum of 36 buttons on a menu

page, it's best not to overwhelm the viewer with a mass of options. It is preferable to limit the choices on the first screen and provide submenus for access, especially if you have a lot of content. This can also provide the user with a sense of anticipation and excitement, especially if you have teaser graphics, button transitions, or motion menus on each screen. Driving the user in a linear direction will also lead to less confusion.

A balance needs to be drawn, however, over the amount of submenu options you provide. You don't want to keep your viewer from your content any longer than necessary. As a general rule, try to provide your user with access to your content with the least amount of clicks on the remote control.

In most cases, menus require you to move over options and press Enter to select them, but you can make buttons even more intelligent by using the auto-activate option. This can be authored into the menu in applications such as Adobe Encore DVD or Ulead DVD Workshop to activate a navigation function when the user selects the

Above: *In menu design, too much choice is as bad as too little. In this case, a lack of structure means that all the options go on the one main menu, resulting in a bewildering mass of buttons that no viewer will be able to make sense of. While the simple layout will make selection fairly easy, it's too crowded and too complicated.*

relevant button with the remote control. This feature is commonly used for arrow buttons or to reveal extra invisible elements, known in the industry as 'Easter eggs'.

Your menu can be made even more intuitive by linking to submenus when a button is auto-activated. The downside of this slick bit of navigation is that your menu becomes more complicated, so it is best avoided if the content or intended audience doesn't warrant or expect such creativity.

Feedback

Good interface design thinking dictates that the user or viewer receives instant notification that their interaction has had some effect. On the DVD menu, this feedback takes the form of buttons that are highlighted when selected or activated, or both. Highlights are commonly enabled by using the subpicture overlay layer, but these have a limited colour depth. Button transitions – motion graphic or audio sequences that play when a button is clicked – are also useful providers of feedback, but these also have problems associated with them. Steer clear of peppering your menu with pointless transitions as what is meant as helpful feedback can become simply irritating.

Motion

Menus that include moving footage are known as motion menus. The way to create such dynamic screens has been well covered elsewhere in this book, but there are a few principles to bear in mind when considering their design. Remember that motion menus have to follow the same design conventions as still menus and must be as compliant in terms of aspect ratio and broadcast safe colours. You can also make sure that the motion only begins after the menu options are displayed so as to focus on the key elements in the hierarchy, i.e. the navigation.

Motion can also help to make your menus user-friendly. You can use transitions to smooth the break between menus, so smoothing the cut. However, such transitions should be constructed as carefully as possible to avoid what is know as 'seamy' breaks, where the video or audio pauses or mutes during the transition.

Menu intro sequences can help to add life to your menu, but they may also distance the viewer from the content. Some authoring packages allow the DVD to skip any long motion introduction sequence if they detect that the viewer has already been to the menu before, so be sure to consider implementing this function in your design.

The good thing about motion elements is that they provide a dynamic experience for the user. Use them wisely – always give your viewer a choice to avoid them and click through to the content as fast as possible. Don't use motion menus, menu intros, and button transitions when the target audience will not welcome this kind of eye candy.

Menu intro sequences can help to add life to your menu, but they may also distance the viewer from the content

Left: *This is better. The grouping of options into four submenus might be arbitrary, but the cleaner layout makes the options clearer and the menu much easier to use.*

Limitations of DVD

Before you start work on your menu, you should take into account some limiting factors that arise due to the nature of TV hardware, the DVD format, and colour technology. While they may not be relevant to your first attempts at authoring, it is best to be aware of these limitations so that you are prepared to take on more professional menu creation.

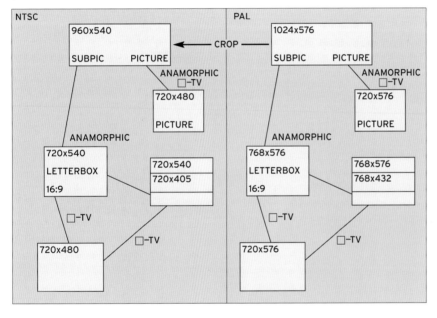

Above: *Professional DVD design studios like Abbey Road Interactive (ARI) have a complicated set of rules to follow for PAL and NTSC graphics, sizes, and conversions. The basic idea is that since computers and* *TVs have pixels with different dimensions, designers should work purely in computer-style square pixels until the last moment, and only convert to TV pixels immediately before the files are delivered to the* *authors. The ARI designers always design within the NTSC safe areas, even when designing for PAL. This allows them to convert to NTSC more easily.*

Subpicture limitations

As we have seen in previous chapters, the typical static DVD menu is usually made up of a layered Adobe Photoshop (or similar) file or separate image files. The background layer contains the static background of the menu, while the subpicture layer, which lies on top, contains any button highlights. The key thing to remember is that the subpicture layer is non-aliased so text should not be used. The simpler the subpicture image, the better the menu will look. Subpictures can only be composed of four colours: white (R:255, G:255, B:255), black (0,0,0), red (255,0,0) and blue (0,0,255), so take this into account (and the fact that one of the four colours will be the background of the subpicture layer) when you are designing. This is particularly relevant if you are intending to pass the menu on to a commercial DVD mastering house or you are a designer working in a professional DVD authoring environment.

Text and line art

Text should always be used with care when designing anything for an interlaced screen. The minimum text size should be 14 point, and sans serif fonts are preferable. Due to the size of the screen, you will only be able to fit 10–15 lines of text within the title safe area, and in any case you should avoid filling your menu with text.

Right: *This photograph is a bad choice as the basis for a menu background. It is relatively busy, featuring both people and landscape elements. You can tell from the grid that the photo is badly positioned within safety areas. The person on the edge of the frame would be largely cropped on a television screen.*

When working with line art and other graphics, be sure to avoid thin lines and objects with small details as this will cause flicker. You can anti-alias the background to avoid this but be aware that you can't apply anti-aliasing to the subpicture layer.

Player vs PC

Normal DVDs have limited scope for interactivity. As discussed before, you need to remember that unless your viewer is watching your DVD on a personal computer, they will be using a remote control with a TV. Their movement is far more limited than if they were using a mouse, being restricted to up, down, left, and right. This makes navigation simple, but can cause problems if you intend your DVD to be played on both platforms. Avoid overlapping buttons. This is a big problem, especially when the DVD is played on a computer. The mouse pointer will be confused by button overlap areas, causing it to jump and act erratically.

Safe colours

Images have to be created using either PAL-safe or NTSC-safe RGB colours. The choice is, of course, dependent on where you expect your DVD to be shown, but if there is a chance of international use, it is always safer to limit your palette to the less forgiving NTSC-safe range. Any background images should be at least 24-bit RGB colour. You can use Photoshop to convert any project images that originated from a CMYK print source into video-friendly RGB, and then make use of the Photoshop *NTSC Color* filter to get your palette working within the NTSC-safe range.

Safe areas

Keep all text and any buttons within the title safe area to compensate for any discrepancies with the scanning system used by TV monitors. The action safe area is considered to be 5 percent from the edge (648 x 432) while title safe is considered to be 10 percent from the edge (576 x 384), but generally speaking, you should keep all crucial information 70 pixels from the sides and 50 pixels from top and bottom. Users of the latest version of Photoshop can specify that any new documents be created in the correct dimensions by choosing the correct preset document size.

Planning the menu

Planning is the key factor in making a DVD menu a slick, professional-looking production, while lack of planning can result in a confusing mess. Consider your content and audience, create a structure, and stick to it. Remember that the menu is there for a purpose and you'll find yourself with an effective result.

Below: *You can create a simple flowchart of the relationships between options, buttons, and menu screens to work out the hierarchy of your menu elements. Using charting software,* *such as ConceptDraw Pro by CS Odessa (shown here) makes it easy to organize your menu in a logical manner. A careful look at this stage can also show up any omissions in your menu plan.*

Know your content

Look at the content you have to work with, decide who is going to be watching the DVD, and start thinking about the level of complexity of your menu. Take notes of all timings, sounds (especially if you are missing some audio), and the amount of photographs or other material you have at your disposal. You might also have to scan in some artwork, invitations, or other supplementary items. Will you be including multi-angle shots or additional audio options? Consider how you will get hold of this material. You can author multiple video and audio streams in a non-linear video-editing package such as Avid Xpress DV or Adobe Premiere Pro, but you need the source material in the first place and you may need to purchase some additional software. Remember also that a DVD disc, while more spacious than a CD, is not infinite. It's easy to go over your limit, so keep tabs on all your content sizes.

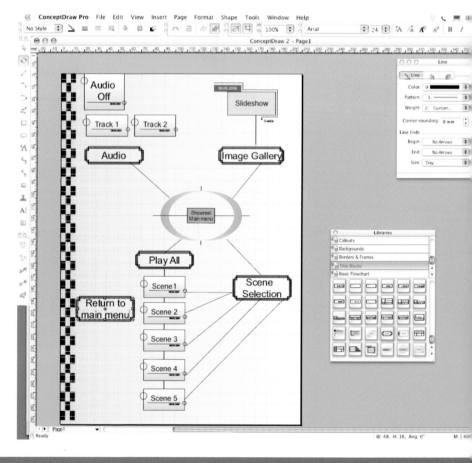

Thunderbirds DVD

All subpictures are at 60% black and work by concealing options that aren't selected.

Superfeatures. Each DVD has a factfile and a feature. Swap the images to suit the content.

Factfiles have up to three pages each, so there are two page buttons and a next/back file option.

DVD-ROM page. To update for each DVD, swap the background image and text to suit the ROM illustration.

Identify the theme or genre of the DVD you want to create and try to find similar professional titles from which you can take inspiration. Don't restrict yourself to blockbuster movies – look at documentaries, advertising showreels, product catalogues, or even some wedding DVDs. Once you begin looking at DVDs with a critical eye, even the most mundane content can gain a whole new dimension. Take mental notes and learn the good and bad points of interface design at first hand.

Know your audience

How technically-astute is your intended audience? You might want your DVD to start playing immediately, in which case a menu is still useful as a backup for navigating the disc, or you might want to provide as many interactive elements as you can – options for foreign languages perhaps, multiple angle shots, or selectable audio tracks.

Where will your DVD be played? On a PC or a TV? There are considerations in both cases in terms of interface design, navigation, interactivity, and button placement. You can also add non-AVI material to a DVD that is intended for PC use, such as PDF documents and Web

links. This DVD-ROM section takes up space, too, so remember to work that into your resources plan.

Think about accessibility. Your audience may be disabled in some way, so take into account basic design rules for creating accessible content (see page 176 for more on this subject).

Create a hierarchy

Like any good presentation or news story, you should attempt to give the viewer an overview of the main points of your menu first, followed up by an exploration of various menus branching off it. This provides structure and establishes the hierarchy of content. You should also allow the viewer to use the first menu to the full – an obvious method is to include a standard Play Movie or Play All option and links to various submenus.

Above: *This storyboard for a series of Thunderbirds DVDs by Abbey Road Interactive shows a main menu and the various submenus, with instructions for any significant options and features. The main menu has a live text layer that can be altered for each disc. Enough space had to be set to accommodate the longest possible combination of letters and words. Clips from the episodes will be played in specially designed frames or windows.*

You can use a simple flowchart sketch or organizational software to determine the hierarchy of your menus, starting with the main functions and branching and connecting subfunctions accordingly. Very soon you'll have a chart showing the main menu elements and the relationships between them. You can then group related items together to form the bones of your submenu screens and you'll know which elements to make bigger or more prominent, based on their position in the hierarchy.

Visualize your menu

Once you have your menu skeleton, the best thing to do is to draft out your ideas for various menus on a scrap of paper. Are you including a photo-gallery or slideshow? How should this be presented? What about subtitles and other information? Will you be including multiangle shots? You'll probably need a separate menu for this, in which case how should that look? What about audio options – alternate tracks, voiceovers, commentary, and foreign languages? Keep to a maximum of six buttons per screen so as not to confuse the viewer.

Try to pre-empt how viewers will interact with the menu. Could you make it simpler? Think about what they will use most and plan to make it the most obvious button or element on the menu. Again, make sure that you've included all the important options on the main screen.

Now you can flesh this out into a storyboard, or series of linked sketches, that show more detail, as well as the interactive side of the menu. Include timings, audio, graphics, any motion menus, and transitions. Storyboards are also a good way to visualize your working menu and confer with clients about the direction it is going, before you start authoring.

Fleshing out the details

Aim for a unified look to your menu screens and decide on this as early as possible. Having a central graphical design is a good way to go, with the positions and look of your various navigational elements being repeated over consecutive screens. Detail these consistent designs in your storyboard for yourself and other people working on the project to remember.

Motion elements

Make sure you have given thought to the duration and behaviours of any animated or dynamic elements of your menu. Now is the time to specify timings and any sequences of motion graphics. These

Left: *For the O Brother, Where Art Thou? DVD release, Abbey Road Interactive created a fully animated main menu followed by a series of transitions that lead to still menus. This image shows the sequence near the end of the triggered animation as the next menu is wiped onto the screen.*

Left and above: *This outdoor sports DVD menu contains the hallmarks of a simple but effective design, including a unified look, a central graphic design, a limited number of options per screen, and a clear indication of selection. Note, however, that the text on the submenu screen could prove too small for some TV sets to display with sufficient clarity.*

can be video clips, but more often in professional studios, designers will use software like After Effects to create motion elements.

Menu access timings

Many designers include animated sequences between menu screens, and especially as an introduction to the main screen. This main intro delay should be kept to a minimum – 3 seconds at most. It should also have a skip function built in. The DVD standard allows you to program discs to remember if the viewer has seen the intro movie, and it is good practice to ensure the intro is skipped automatically if a viewer returns to this screen in the same session.

Designers can also specify animated clips when buttons are pressed, to enhance the viewer experience and provide feedback. These animated transitions between submenus should be very rapid, with a maximum 1 second delay. They give designers a chance to be creative and some excellent work has been done in this field. However, viewers will very quickly become tired of waiting, no matter how fantastic your transitions seem on first viewing. Avoid adding transitions between important submenus for this reason.

Depending on the DVD player, a delay between menus is sometimes unavoidable. The player scans through the hierarchy for the right screen and will drill down through 'nested' or layered folders. Make sure your menu structure is as 'flat' as possible and avoid nesting too many folders within each other.

Motion menus

Should you include motion in your menus? Moving images are undeniably eyecatching and will provide a focal point for any menu. It's for this very reason that you need to be careful when using motion menus – the whole point is to direct the viewer to the content, so make sure your navigation buttons are also prominent.

It may become irritating for the viewer to watch the same sequence in a loop, but avoid making the footage in your motion menus too long – 30 seconds is a good upper level. Video takes up a lot of space on a DVD and if you have too many transitions you can run into problems fitting your main content on the disc.

Using Photoshop to create layouts

Adobe Photoshop CS is a highly useful and versatile tool for creating DVD menus. Competing products such as Macromedia Fireworks and Corel Photo Paint also offer layer-based image editing, but here we'll be looking at building a simple project using the Adobe application, taking advantage of its integrated features for DVD menu creation. While we will be using the application on Mac OS X, all tools and conventions also apply to the Windows version.

Below: *Like most professional DVD menus, this layout was created using Adobe Photoshop before the authoring stage.*

Creating a menu for a ski-trip DVD

Let's create some basic still menus for a homemade DVD based around a skiing and snowboarding trip to Saalbach, Austria. As the first part of our planning, we'll take a look at our potential DVD contents. We have three edited pieces of footage, a number of photographs for a gallery, and some audio tracks. So, overall the DVD will require four main interfaces, with the audio playing over the still images. We can break this down into a step-by-step process.

Main menu

1 The main menu will be designed around a photograph. We can use Photoshop's *Browser* to judge the most appropriate and provide an overview of all the images. The images are judged on relevant content, space in which to include titles and options, as well as general aesthetic qualities.

This photo was chosen as a basis for the first menu because of its dramatic lighting, good composition, and potential for overlaying type. It's relatively simple and would work well on TV. Additionally, it doesn't give too much away and suggests that there is content to be discovered.

2 The photo was too dark so the *Levels* are adjusted to achieve a more desirable balance of contrast. The image is then placed in a PAL compatible document (768 x 576 pixels) and positioned within the PAL safety area as shown. Always make sure that all relevant imagery is within the action safe area and generally within the tighter title safe area.

SAALBACH04
FOOTAGE
GALLERY
AUDIO

3 Some type layouts are tried next. This one uses a simple Helevetica Bold that sits quite well. The font is 36 point, which is large enough for there to be no problem with legibility. A white colour is used for the title to differentiate it from any selectable options. However, it is slightly dull and doesn't interact with the image.

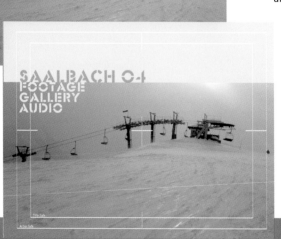

SAALBACH 04
FOOTAGE
GALLERY
AUDIO

4 The text is removed and a flat colour block is inserted to provide an area of negative space for the type to sit on. This increases clarity and is enhanced by using a muted colour that doesn't clash with the photograph. A new font, Glaser Stencil was chosen, set at 48pt for the title and 36pt for the options, with a leading value of 24. This font is more dynamic and adds to the overall feel. The flat colour area allows the title to be placed outside of the image and the options placed within. This positioning, along with the opposing colours, reinforces the difference between titles and options.

5 The menu still doesn't feel right, with the presence of the colour block reducing the drama of the image and the lighting in the sky. The block is discarded and a new font called BIN Bold is used at a chunky size of 54 pt with a leading of 26 pt. This brings the lines of type closer together, which makes it self-contained and more aesthetically pleasing. A white colour for the title contrasts with a dark colour for the 04, while the dramatic lighting behind reinforces the contrast. The options are given their own more muted colour. This font works because it feels modern and its stark blocky shape complements the curves and sweeps of the image behind, making the type stand out. The type is moved to the centre so that it interacts better with the image and works well with the area of detail at the top of the ski lift. As the eyes are drawn to this point automatically, it makes sense to put the information here.

6 The image contrast is a little strong and could do with being more harmonized with the type colours. Using the dark grey and the light grey as foreground and background colours, a *Gradient Map* is applied. This allocates the two colours to the black/white luminance of the image resulting in a screen-printed look that is more subtle and sits better with the text. To reintroduce some of the original colour and contrast the *Gradient Map* layer is set to 70% *Opacity* over the original to create a compromise.

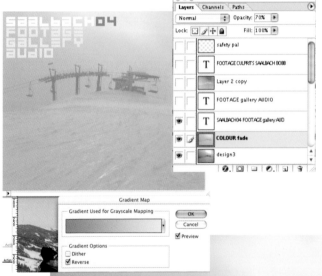

7 The final design possesses good type legibility, obvious usability, and is also aesthetically pleasing. This menu will set the tone for the three submenus that will flow from it. Simple white lines are used for the subpicture overlays. These rest to the right of the options and reach as far as the title above, so creating a rectangular area. This kind of simple shape is ideal for the hard edged (aliased) nature of the subpicture and will not distort.

Footage menu

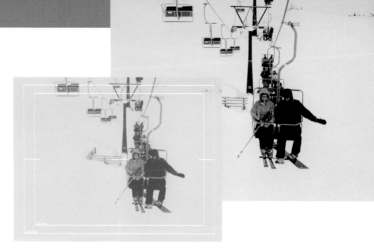

1 This image, chosen for the footage menu, has good composition and a lot of blank space to use for options. It also feels like a companion piece to the main menu image, continuing the ski lift theme. The same *Gradient Map* colours that were applied to the main menu are applied once again. Again, the *Opacity* was dropped to 70% to reveal the original image below. The image sits well within the safety areas, but there are details, like the chair top left, that may get cropped.

2 As there is no more image, the scene cannot be scaled down any further. To solve this, a white border is added to the submenus so that the photo can be moved down to within the safety area, without being awkwardly cropped. The white border may or may not show up on some televisions, but it will appear on a PC, so this way the image is optimized for both formats.

3 The title of the DVD is applied in the same font and size as the main menu, but the colours are reversed for Saalbach and 04. These little signifiers help separate the main menu from a submenu. It is decided that colour will be used for the subtitle and options in the submenus. The best way to find a colour in the image that will work is to use the *Color Picker*. Here a muted cyan from the jacket of the girl on the ski lift was chosen, as the colour will flow with the image.

4 There are three footage clips to choose, so it is decided to create a visual layout, using a screengrab from each edit as the selections. The menu would become too busy if further explanatory type were added to the boxes to explain the content. A main menu button is added to the bottom right of the screen. This will remain in a consistent position throughout all the submenus for ease of use. The colour matches the title to link this option visually with the main menu.

5 The video windows are removed and replaced with type selections, to better suit the composition of the image. The layout is now dominated by the strong central line of the ski lift support column and everything branching out from this. The text is right justified to enforce this. The option font is set at 36 pt, as this also differentiates the submenu from the main menu, with the hierarchy of the menus reflected by the font sizes. The subpictures reflect those on the main menu but have been extended all the way to the borders as this was found to work better in design terms.

Gallery menu

1 This photograph was chosen because of its strong composition and the space available for options. The figures in the picture are positioned well for a menu, and are essentially strong but simple shapes. As before, the *Gradient Map* colours were applied and the *Opacity* dropped to 70%.

2 A border is applied for the same reasons as for the *Footage* menu, to get everything required within safety but to avoid having cropped edges on display. Windows are used to display the three galleries to choose from (a, b, and c). The windows work in design terms because of the amount of free space available on the right. The lack of written explanations of the gallery contents further serves to simplify the design. The muted red lines underneath will be used for the positions of the selection subpictures. The Main button remains in its bottom-right location, while it and the title option are also aligned with the heads of the figures. This all adds to the composition.

3 The title and windows were moved to the right as they were unnecessarily close to the figure on the left, so giving the design more space to breathe. The subpictures were assigned a white colour over the red lines under the gallery window.

Audio menu

1 This is a good photo to use for the Audio menu as, again, it has simplicity, good composition, and space for options. The same colours were used for the *Gradient Map*, but this time the reverse button was applied. However, the effect felt too inconsistent, so this option was discarded and the menu was treated as the two submenus before.

2 This menu presents four audio tracks for the user to select. As they are tunes associated with the Apres Ski, the Apres Ski Tunes subhead needs to go somewhere on the menu. The first idea was to fit the text into the mountain with a right justification opposing the left justification of the submenu title. But this seemed to fight the natural composition of the image. Consequently, the same justification was applied to the subhead. The smaller font still separates it sufficiently from the main titles.

3 The options here are laid out in such a way as to match the flow of the skiers down the hill. The eye naturally follows the options down and eventually over to the Main option in its bottom-right position.

4 As the type follows the skiers down, the subpictures are extended to pick out a particular figure on the slope. This is a playful example of the use of subpictures and exploits the composition of the image in a constructive way.

Creating a look to match the movie

The style of a menu is very important, especially when you want to create a unified mood to your DVD. It's no use laying down a menu with wacky animated options over a serious corporate portfolio. Always aim to complement the main content on the disc. Achieving this requires some thought and planning.

Below: *This is a very simple menu based on a template in Studio Pro. Simple, subdued colours, delicate fonts, and the two rings in soft focus give the wedding screen a* *romantic feel, while the central image leaves no doubt as to whose wedding DVD it is. Basic navigation is provided by clear, no-nonsense style buttons.*

First you need to decide just what sort of DVD you are creating. Is it a wedding video, or a pop video for a band? Get the concept firmly in place before you start to think about designing the look and feel of your menu. Your next task is to define your target audience. Is it members of your family? Or is it potential clients, possibly in a foreign country? A great many factors need to be taken into account. Design the look of the menu with your audience in mind, or you run the risk of alienating them or offending them before your DVD even begins. On the other hand, if this is a completely personal project, why not throw caution to the wind and experiment?

Family entertainment

DVD has taken the place of VHS, the slide show, and the Super 8 film projector in the living rooms of the world. Holiday footage and video of family anniversaries and other celebrations are ideal for DVD.

The format is durable, multi-region compatible, and easy to send around the globe. When designing a menu for the family DVD, remember to keep things simple – some people don't even know

how to set the clock on the VCR, so hidden extras and confusing navigation are probably not a good idea. Traditional design would seem to be a safe bet: the clichés of wedding bells and horseshoes

Left: *A DVD menu design can help transform holiday movies by giving them a more interesting travel-log feel. In this case, the menu uses colour gradients and an appropriate font to create a suitable atmosphere that ties together the holiday video footage.*

for marriages, balloons, candles, and cakes for birthdays, beaches and sunsets for holidays are all used regularly for good reason. However, that doesn't mean that you need to rely on them. You can give them a new twist by matching the tone and style of your menu design to the individual style of the wedding. Just remember: the audience is more interested in the content than your graphic design skills, so don't waste your time creating an avant-garde work of art. Prosumer DVD authoring packages are geared precisely towards this market, so take advantage of the assets they supply.

Above right and right: *There are several approaches you can take to wedding DVD menus. The tried and tested design includes flowery fonts, soft focus, romantic colours and an awful lot of clip art, but you can also take a less busy, more elegant route. Just because the service is traditional, it doesn't mean you can't include animation and transitions to add interest. The important thing is to maintain a consistent look and feel across the various menus and submenus, and use common navigation systems.*

Advertising your services

Corporate DVD

If you are intending to send out your work on DVD to potential business contacts, you have to ensure that you make the right impression from the start. Flashy graphics, cutting-edge navigation, and pounding music beats will probably make most corporate viewers turn off, long before you get your main message across. If your business image is smooth and professional, your DVD menu should reflect this. It doesn't mean your DVD should be unadventurous and dull, but a more basic, user-friendly approach is advised. Keep navigation to a minimum, get to the message and main content as swiftly as possible. Time is money where corporate applications are concerned, so keep your menu as clean and efficient as possible.

Creative business

If your area of work is in design, animation, or any of the creative industries, however, you'll want to show you are on the cutting edge. Progressive menu design is key, but loud animated menus and clever composited graphics can turn off clients in this area, too, especially if you overuse an effect that a thousand designers have used before. Advertising agencies and design studios have a vested interest in producing eye-catching menus and interactive designs so take a look at a few of these for inspiration. But remember to tailor any designs to your own requirements – aside from avoiding plagiarism, you need to make sure the design is relevant to the rest of your creative output. As a rule, you should always keep it as simple and original as possible.

Below right: These are menus for a DVD showreel for Mission Television, a London-based production company. The brief was to be simple and clear and to design the screen in the style of the Mission logo.

There is no main menu as such on this disc because each menu has the same design. The contents are laid out to the left, and when each is displayed, the subcontents of each section are laid out on the right. This utilizes a still menu concept – a very user-friendly, no frills interface. The design has a

corporate feel to it, with a cool blue and grey colour scheme and a graphic and functional menu layout. This system makes accessing the content easier and dispenses with unnecessary imagery

or indulgent animations. The subpictures cover the options in flat colour at 50% opacity, revealing the option you have chosen and allowing its true colour to be seen underneath.

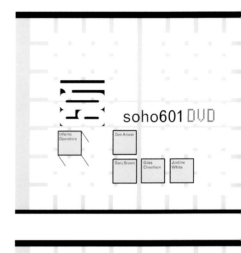

Top: After a brief menu intro, this clean, simple, but interesting menu screen appears, introducing the work of film and TV production house Soho 601. Based in the middle of London's media heartland, the design evokes a city plan, with buildings and streets seen from above, and also a pixelated image.

Above: The submenu that takes the viewer to the work of the facility's video-effects team carries on the same themes as the main menu. The button to return to the main menu is not instantly obvious. It is, in fact, the large 601 logo.

Movies

It's not likely that the job of producing the DVD of a feature film would go anywhere but to a professional DVD studio, but there is nothing to stop you giving your own short film the Hollywood treatment. A good design rule is to reference elements of the film and replicate them in the menu – try to make the menu both relevant and aesthetically pleasing. If done with taste and restraint, this will give the project a more professional appearance.

Above: *This is a single-menu DVD created for a short film. A very simple layout, it takes elements of the film and uses them as a basis for the design.*

The designer was given a still from the film and produced an illustration taking the main characters and the wall behind as the focus.

The subpictures are simple squares, an easy shape for hard edging. The delineated safety area shows the expanded areas available to work in on a 16:9 project.

Left: *This menu is a good example from a home movie on DVD. The two main films Gelatinous Maw and Maw Power are zero-budget, humorous horror pastiches about 'psychotic jam', so the menu was designed with that in mind. It is a very simple menu with two options and a hidden button. The options are laid out around the facial features with the title above and the films on either side – very clean*

and obvious on a white background. This way the menu is balanced and not weighted one way or the other. Scratchy lines were designed for the subpicture. These fit the horror theme and are also easy to do hard-edged (because of the aliased nature of the layer). If you use the Pencil tool and switch off the anti-aliasing you get instant scratchy lines. The arrow beneath the mouth is the hidden

button that will go to a third movie on the disc.

Below: *A 10-second animated menu intro revealing the main cast and finishing on the main menu at the end was used to add a sense of mystery and menace.*

Music video

Menu design, especially if you are designing for a client, depends greatly on budget considerations. Music videos are notoriously underfunded and it's likely that the DVD project will be, too. However, large record companies are putting their artists' material out on DVD more and more, so the market is there and sizable investment in the project is possible. If the recording artist and the style of the music warrants it, you can have flashy experimental animation and layered interactive graphics. Hidden menu extras and 'Easter eggs' are also popular, as are Web links. Another consideration is options for foreign languages, particularly if the project is for a musician who is internationally recognized.

You may have to bid for design work. The normal practice is to develop storyboards for approval by the client. Often these will be full-sized images of the menu and design elements, which take a lot of time and effort to prepare. If the bid is unsuccessful, there is very little chance of financial return.

This Is Stina Nordenstam: Initial design

This DVD was created at Abbey Road Interactive and contains 11 Stina Nordenstam videos. As occasionally happens, the team were given no artwork or information about the artist but were asked to come up with a storyboard showing potential menu designs.

Below left: *The various elements were recycled from menu to menu. This was done so that the team could save time and get across the idea and feel without investing too much in a design that might eventually be completely altered when more information became available, as was indeed the case.*

Below: *The initial concept was an unusual futuristic abstract design featuring 3D rendered organic pods and references to cities and strange landscapes. The 3D elements were created and rendered in Infini-D then exported to Photoshop.*

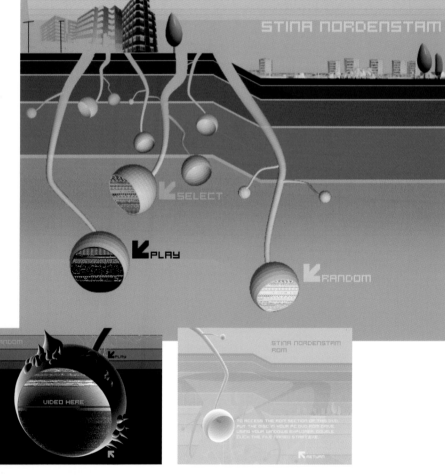

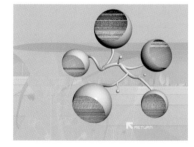

This Is Stina Nordenstam: Second Design

The second design took a different tack, with a theme based on Victorian circus posters.

Below left: *The new circus theme featured ornate styling, performing animals, and playbill style fonts.*

Below: *The final design featured a symmetrical/mirrored design with circus elements positioned around a central hub. The title font was created with a combination of three Victorian style fonts to create a stylized hybrid. Each element around the central hub represents a video or another option such as credits.*

Left: *The unusual navigation on this DVD means that there are mostly no subpictures. Instead, each selectable item has its own menu design made up of a still image. The designs are essentially the same image, but with a different background colour and a particular circus element highlighted with the name of the video under a screenshot in the centre. The user hits left or right on the remote control to make the menu change to another still image. When the user reaches the video they want, pressing select will play that video. This unconventional method means that any audio attached will be immediately cut off as the user switches, but if the menus are silent, it is a very effective way to bypass any unappealing subpictures and inject variety into the design.*

Fonts, backgrounds, and colours

When you have decided on a look for your menu and have gone some way to planning it, it's time to take a closer look at the design elements that make up the menu screens. When looking for images to use as menu backgrounds, consider their composition and the colours that make up the picture. This will determine your choice of colours, and the design of elements such as graphics, lines, and fonts that you'll add to the image to create a serviceable and attractive menu.

Above right and right: *This is a DVD single for 'Crystal' by New Order, created at Abbey Road Interactive. The photographs used as backgrounds for the main menu, audio, and live excerpts menus were stark black and white figure shots. They were also portrait, which is a problem for the landscape format of television. To overcome this, the designer introduced a flat block of complementary colour to sit to the left* *of the images and contain all the options. This enabled more of the image to be included on the screen and presented a user-friendly, clear interface. It would have been difficult to maintain consistency throughout if the text was laid directly onto the photograph. The limited duotone palette used for fonts, backgrounds, and subpictures sets a balance for the series of menus.*

Colour

Colour should be used with care. You can use it to create mood and harmony, or you can give your viewers a real headache. Colour can express the themes and direction of your content in subconscious ways. With conservative colours, you can put across a business-like theme, or give a wacky face to your content with loud, cartoon graphics.

You can add visual interest to your menu by using contrasting colours. This approach can also show the hierarchy of elements in your scene and distinguish between dissimilar elements. If two elements have a different purpose or are otherwise unrelated, the use of strong

For the DVD of U2 Go Home the ARI designer decided the colour scheme would be based on that of the Irish flag, drawing on the homecoming theme of the concert.

However off-white was applied to the background photo using a gradient map because full white can create problems on television screens. It can appear too bright

and warp text or images. A RGB value of 235, 235, 235, which is considered a safe white, was used instead.

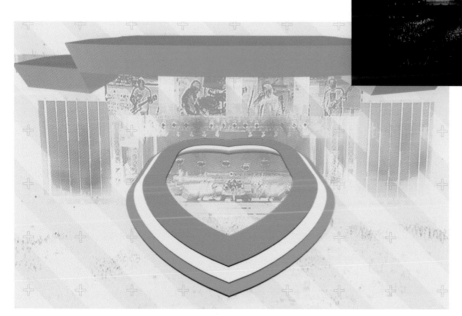

contrasting colours will highlight this disparity. It is not just colour that can be used in contrasting fashion. All menu elements – text, line strength, even spatial positioning and audio can be contrasted to suggest relationships and lift a menu to a more professional level.

Some designers set a limit on the number of colours they use, and it might suit you to assign yourself a palette of three colours and stick to it throughout your project. As well as ensuring consistency, this will help to preserve balance and harmony in your interface.

Keep it safe

Always think of colour in terms of broadcast-safe palettes. Safe or legal colour limits should be adhered to when creating DVD menus as well as the content they serve.

Televisions don't have the same width of colour range as computer monitors, so some menus that use fully saturated examples of red, blue, or green may cause distortions. This is known as bleeding, when the colour from one over-saturated pixel overflows into neighboring pixels. An average family TV usually has the colour saturation set at a high level so this problem is exacerbated. Bright yellows and reds are notable culprits for distortion, but all menu graphics should have colours firmly below a luminance value of 230. TV images can also have a problem with too much black and white – if the levels are too high for the TV, clipping can occur, resulting in a loss of detail. To prevent this, use the *Levels* function in Photoshop to adjust the peaks for both black and white to within

safe limits (16 is the level for video black and a peak level of 235 should be set for video white) to reduce the contrast. Graphics that share similar luminance values will be difficult to view if a user is colour-blind, so think about contrasting colours when designing for usability.

The *NTSC Color* filter in Photoshop will be able to remedy most of the ills associated with colour while the *Soft Proof* function can show you a preview of how your menu will look on a TV screen. You can set it for PAL or NTSC proofs.

If you are not already acquainted with RGB values, explore the subject using Photoshop or a similar image editor. Red, green, and blue, the colours that make up the pixels in a video picture, are given luminance values that correspond to their varying strength in the pixel. These values are allocated out of a maximum of 255, and the combination of the three values determines the final colour of the pixel.

Another issue to be aware of is bit-depth; the amount of colour data that is available for each pixel. The standard DVD specification that all DVD players conform to requires that subpictures should be 8-bit RGB with only four colours. As the background colour is always white (255, 255, 255), this actually leaves only three colours to be used. On a related note, most commercial DVD authoring houses require background images to be prepared in 24-bit RGB.

Right: *The text used for the title here is a Helvetica font with a Chromed Satin style from the Photoshop Styles palette. The option text is in Sand font with a drop shadow applied. The title gets lost on the background due to the blue of the style blending with the sky. The options are clumsily dropped onto the figures in the photograph. The two fonts and styles clash and do nothing to enhance the image behind.*

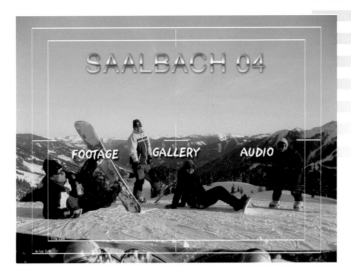

Lines and patterns

Interlaced scan lines on TV screens can cause mayhem with an otherwise well ordered and constructed menu design. Thin lines will judder on screen because they only occupy one scan line, so make sure they are at least three pixels thick or anti-aliased (remember that the subpicture layer cannot be anti-aliased). Applying a blur effect, including a *Gaussian Blur* or a slight vertical *Motion Blur* will do the trick, but make sure the blur radius or distance is very small. Use equivalent filters in After Effects or other compositing tools. This softening effect is barely visible on TV but it generally fixes the problem. It is also best to avoid designs with patterns such as dots or alternating chess squares as these nearly always jitter, but if you do use them, make sure they have been softened considerably.

Text

As we have seen, designers usually use contrasting colours for text and the background. It helps make the one stand out from the other. However, you should try to avoid using outrageous colour combinations in your DVD menus unless this is the precise effect you are going for. Bright green on a lemon-yellow background is unlikely to win you any design prizes and it is simply difficult to read, which defies the whole point of having text on your menu in the first place. Even black on white can cause

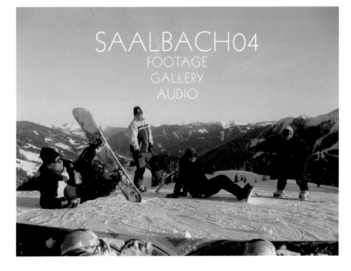

Left: *An image we've seen before, but this time using a font called Kabel Light throughout, set at 60pt for the title and 30pt for options. This font works better with the image: it's cleaner and has a gracefulness that matches the mountains behind. But overall, the menu is not successful. The font is large enough, but the lightness of the type lines may get lost on TV screens while the very thin horizontal lines will definitely jitter on television.*

problems when used with a serif font, as the higher the contrast between the foreground text and the background colour, the greater the jitter effect, thanks to the additional problem of interlaced TV screens. Conversely, if the text colour and background have too close a luminance value, the graphics may get muddy and confused on TV, leading to an unreadable or ugly menu.

Left: *This image has a lot of detail in the distant background, while the darker shadows to the top right could be suitable for a light font type. A font called Fructosa (title set at 60pt, options at 30pt) is used to give a 'grungy' feel. However, with no real structure to the menu, the type feels like it has been dropped on at random.*

Failed menus

Several components that work with the theme you have chosen may fail to gel in a menu. Trial and error and a clear eye for the overall design will see you through, but you may have to completely discard a few attempts along the way.

Right: *Using Photoshop, a Photo Filter effect is applied to the image in an attempt to cool it down and give it a more wintry feel. A new font, Discount Inferno, is used at same point sizes as the Fructosa menu, but the options are staggered in a downward motion, following the figures in the image to try to integrate the type more. Sadly, the font seems ill-considered, and the filter effect makes the colour just too unnatural.*

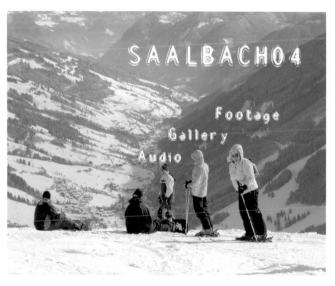

You can create simple variation and define areas of interest by using different typefaces of the same font family, but keep variations and the amount of fonts to a minimum. With any combinations of text colours and typefaces that you use, remember to keep them consistent throughout your menu system. Viewers will get confused if you change the font style or colours with every screen. Try also to avoid cluttering up your screen with too much text – a cleaner menu is more appealing.

Remember that reading text on a screen is hard anyway, so don't cause more problems by using fonts that are too small to read. Any anti-aliased, 24-point sans serif is a good typeface to use, with 16 point being the minimum font size that you should work with in menu design. It's also wise to leave space between the lines and keep them short. Kerning, or spacing between letters, should be kept as wide as possible for onscreen text, but avoid overkill as this can end up looking like

a mistake. Again, remember to keep usability rules in mind, especially in the case of coloured fonts and subtitles. Captioning and subtitling fonts are notoriously hard to read, being limited in their colour palette, and you don't want to make legibility even harder.

Left: *Here's a masterclass in bad menu design. The colours don't work; the background is too vivid; the text isn't bold enough to stand out from the background, and the slimline font and bevel effect don't help. The text isn't lined up properly, and the placement of the buttons, and of the musical note graphic within the buttons, is woefully inconsistent.*

The good news is that it won't take much to improve it. With this menu, the only way is up.

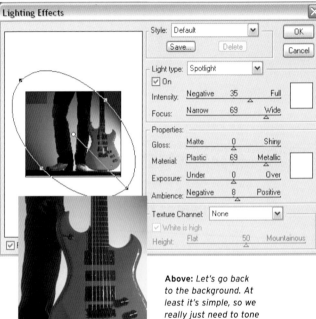

Above: *Let's go back to the background. At least it's simple, so we really just need to tone it down a little. The Spotlight option in Photoshop's Lighting Effects filter takes the emphasis away from the left side of the image – clearing it to make a good background for the menu – but keeps the graphic qualities of the image intact.*

Above: *There's no reason why this design couldn't work with the existing colours, but there are other, more interesting options available. Adjusting the Hue and Saturation of the image (as shown) produces this 'stage-lit' result.*

The text isn't lined up properly, and the placement of buttons is inconsistent

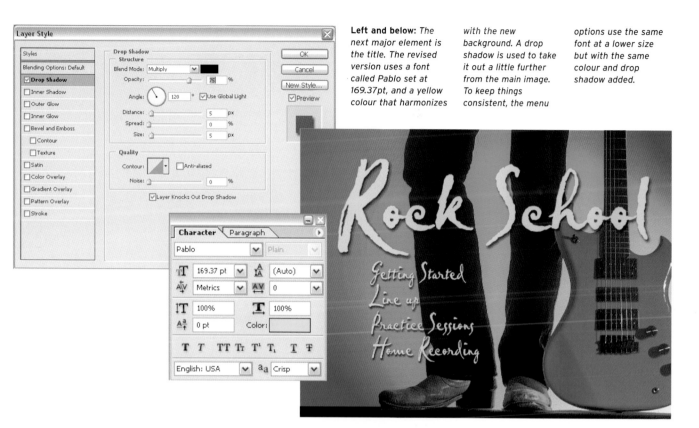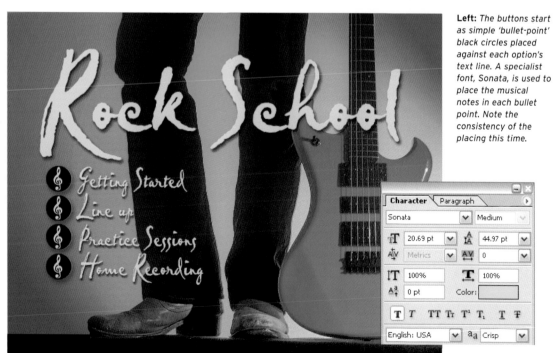

Left and below: *The next major element is the title. The revised version uses a font called Pablo set at 169.37pt, and a yellow colour that harmonizes with the new background. A drop shadow is used to take it out a little further from the main image. To keep things consistent, the menu options use the same font at a lower size but with the same colour and drop shadow added.*

Left: *The buttons start as simple 'bullet-point' black circles placed against each option's text line. A specialist font, Sonata, is used to place the musical notes in each bullet point. Note the consistency of the placing this time.*

Showcase

24

DGP created an all-singing, all-dancing menu for the DVD release of *24*, capturing the signature visual style of the show.

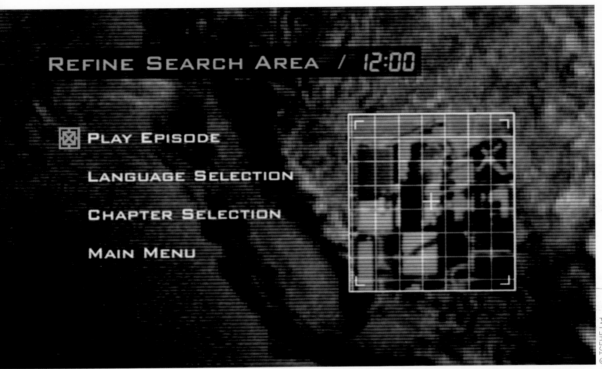

Left: *The hi-tech nature of the 24 TV show, with its use of up-to-the-minute technology, was reflected in the DVD menu's animations, transitions, and overall design. Here's a shot of an episode's submenu, designed to mimic a surveillance satellite computer screen.*

© TCFHE Ltd.

In Twentieth Century Fox's TV hit *24*, we follow the adventures of agent Jack Bauer through a particularly hectic day in his life, hour by hour in real time. DGP's digital artist Kathryn Davey was entrusted with the task of designing the menu for the DVD release. As the program has a distinct visual style, with the narrative unfolding on multiple screens, Kathryn chose to incorporate that look in the DVD's menu. In this way, the menu became a seamless extension of the show, even including the striking countdown sound effect that introduces each episode. Kathryn included multiple short clips from the episodes in each disc's main menu to give the DVD user a taste of the show's content.

It's appropriate, given the program's hi-octane action style, that the DVD menu for *24* is so constantly animated. The animated motion menu emphasizes

Left: *When each disc from the six disc box set is inserted into a DVD player, an introductory sequence plays before the main menu. In this introduction, the numbers flicker and fade up from black to reveal the number 24 that is the show's title, in much the same way that the numbers appear at the beginning of each episode. Getting the menu to mirror the show's opening gives a coherent feel to DVD viewing experience as a whole.*

'You could give the whole film away if you're not careful and you could ruin it.'

the show's sense of excitement and suspense. It contains multiple clips playing in different windows, and flickering digital links inviting the user to click on them.

The trick to good motion menu design is not to show too much content. There is a danger that instead of whetting the viewer's appetite, the menu could spoil their enjoyment. As Kathryn warns: 'You could give the whole film away if you're not careful and ruin it.'

Kathryn's fellow DVD designer, Tim Long, agrees: 'When we first started doing DVD design we used to do a lot of moving menus that included edits from the movie. I didn't like that because you just feel like you've simply watched another trailer.'

Deciding what clips to include in the menu was an important and tricky part of the design process. As Kathryn explains: 'It was an issue with *24* because we were creating the DVD menu as the show was going out in the States, so we were designing things without knowing what the story was going to be like. We were putting characters in our generic design that we didn't even know were going to be alive.'

Left: *As the introduction plays, we hear voiceovers from the episodes on the disc that give clues to the content of the show. A montage of still images and moving clips from the disc's episodes appear in windows within the main interface, mirroring the multi-screen style of the show. As the introductory sequence finishes, four episode numbers appear one by one, accompanied by the characteristic countdown beat that features prominently throughout the show.*

Right: *As the introduction sequence finishes, the numbers indicating the disc's four episodes flicker and flash before settling down. Kathryn explains how the effect on the numbers was created: 'It was actually taken from a library shot of moving water scaled right down. As the water ripples, the highlights on the top of the water glow orange. When keyed on top of the number, you get this glowing electrical feel.'*

Right: *So far, none of the effects that the DVD user is seeing have been created in a DVD authoring package. All this animation is achieved by using Flint to mix together clips from the show and stills from Photoshop to create a hi-tech-looking intro movie. When the introduction sequence finishes, the motion menu plays in a loop, showing a montage of mini clips from the episodes on the disc. The numbers settle down to a simple static read out.*

© TCFHE Ltd.

© TCFHE Ltd.

Left: *Here's the really clever bit. Because of the constraints of authoring DVDs, subpictures are always static overlays that change to indicate that a button has been selected. However, the 24 menu features animated buttons that flicker into life when selected. How is this possible? The effect is achieved by a moving menu background that shows all of the buttons animating at once. The animated numbers are then each masked with their own black subpicture that has a small static number on it. When an episode number is selected, the static subpicture turns transparent to reveal the animated number beneath.*

4
moving pictures

Creative menu ideas

The technical limitations of the DVD format pose some challenges to designers from print or Web backgrounds but, as with any medium, there are also some advantages. DVD was designed to present video media, and the standard supports some exciting ways to showcase moving video and enhance the viewer's interaction with the material. Moving backgrounds and chapter previews are only the start. 3D elements, animations, and complex transitions are all part of the menu designer's palette.

Using motion

As we've discussed, DVD menus don't need to revolve exclusively around Photoshop graphics and static backgrounds. If the theme and intended audience of your DVD warrants it, you can introduce motion. As you will have seen on DVDs from your own collection, or in the showcase examples earlier in this book, motion can take many forms, from a simple animated logo, to buttons that display short video clips, or even full-blown animated backgrounds. This can lift and enliven your menu, giving it a slick, professional feel. Before we go about constructing these animated elements, however, let's take a brief look at some examples of motion menus in various genres.

Using movie clips
O Brother, Where Art Thou?

The DVD for this Coen brothers' film featured a selection of innovative menus by Abbey Road Interactive (ARI) that reflect the strong 1920s styling of the movie, but also take into account the film's sense of humour and character. The designer began by searching the movie for appropriate footage to use as a video clip background for the main menu within a 30-second time frame. This was found near the start of the film, in a comic sequence where the three heroes make their escape through a cornfield. It just needed a little adjustment (*see left*).

Above: *For the main menu of O Brother, Where Art Thou?, the designer treated the footage and boosted the colours, adding additional cloud movement to the sky* to add drama and darken the edges to create a subtle frame for the action. A shrinking, circular fade-to-black effect was added to the beginning and end of the menu to evoke the silent movies of the period. This effect also meant that the designer didn't have to create a perfect loop for the footage.

TRAPPED IN THE SKY

PIT OF PERIL

PERILS OF PENELOPE

TERROR IN NEW YORK CITY

SUPER FEATURES

AUDIO

Below: *The designer of Coldplay Live 2003 used After Effects to create an animated particle effect that seamlessly blended in with the supplied artwork. The particles were masked onto the 2D design and gently blended in to appear as though they were following the lines of the figure. To repeat the cycle, the particles self-generated every few seconds then faded away, giving an overall effect that was very subtle and appropriate to the design.*

COLDPLAY LIVE 2003

CONCERT
TOUR DIARY
EXTRAS

Above: *Andy Potts of ARI created some wonderfully animated 3D elements and background effects for a series of DVDs of the popular Thunderbirds series. Basing the menu theme on the metallic surfaces of the ships and models used in the series, the designer created a 3D model of Thunderbird 1 in Amapi. Textures were created in Photoshop and the model was brought into Infini-D for animating and rendering. A window to the right of the main menu was created to play pieces of footage from the episodes on the disc as they were selected. To add drama, fire was added in the foreground, and 3D rubble, girders, piping, and rocks were set to drop down the screen in front of the rocket, all composited in After Effects.*

Using animation

Sometimes all a designer has to work with are print-based designs and two-dimensional images. For the DVD menu for the release of *Coldplay Live 2003*, Andy Potts, lead designer at ARI, used animated elements to turn 2D designs into a workable format for television and a user-friendly DVD interface.

Using 3D elements

3D applications can literally add another dimension to your menus. Obviously some skill is needed to create 3D models to use as elements, but there are numerous low-cost software applications that can help you produce simple models. A guitar for a music video, a ring for a wedding DVD, a snowboard for the DVD of a winter holiday – all can be made up quickly and easily in accessible software. If you can't do it yourself, you can easily buy a royalty-free model. Fully animated backgrounds are available on the same basis for those who want a completely easy approach to adding motion.

Using movie clips

Adding motion can be a key part of bringing your DVD menu to life. But how do you actually go about it? In basic terms, the main uses of motion in a DVD menu are chapter previews and backgrounds (we'll also cover transitions later on). These are easy to create using your video editing and DVD authoring packages. For the purposes of this example, we'll use iMovie and DVD Studio Pro.

1 Use your editing package to create short preview clips for each chapter. As the clips will loop within the DVD menu window, you can afford to keep their duration short. They won't need to play for long as it's unlikely that the viewer will spend a great deal of time watching the chapter menus. Keeping clips short will also keep file sizes down and save valuable disc space. To create a preview clip in iMovie, double-click on a clip and label it.

Producing chapter previews

As a DVD's content is broken up into chapters (or scenes), it's easy for the user to find a favourite scene, or carry on viewing from where they left off at a previous sitting. You can make it even easier for the DVD user to make an informed decision about which chapter to watch by creating animated chapter previews. These moving clips within the scene menu interface act like mini previews for the chapters.

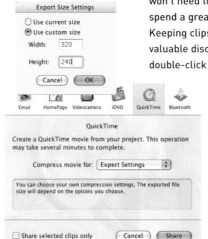

2 Export the clip from iMovie, by going to the main menu and choose *File*, then *Share*. Select the *QuickTime* option. Choose the advanced settings option. This will let you set the exported clip's resolution so that it is smaller than full screen (320 x 240 pixels, for example). This small size is acceptable, as you'll be scaling down the preview in DVD Studio Pro so it fits inside the existing buttons in the DVD chapter menu.

3 In this example, we've already created a chapter menu with still image buttons that hint at the content of the scenes. Subpictures have already been created and each button has been told to target the DVD's relevant chapter marker (see page 60). We don't want to redo any of our settings, but we want to replace the still image with a movie. You can import the preview movies using the *Assets* tab at the bottom centre of the screen.

4 Once you've imported your chapter preview clip into Studio Pro, you are ready to add it to the scene menu. We could drag the clip to an existing preview button. However, the existing buttons are stretched rectangles designed to highlight the still image and the text. The movie clips would fill these buttons, hiding the text and becoming distorted. Click anywhere in the main menu window and draw a more suitably shaped rectangular button.

5 Drag the moving movie clip from the *Assets* tab onto the button you've created. Choose *Set Asset* from the pop-up menu's list of options. The movie will appear inside the button. If you click on the *Simulate* icon, you'll see the preview movie playing within the button you created. Close the *Simulation* window to continue editing. Move the new movie clip button so that it overlaps the still image preview icon from the background graphic.

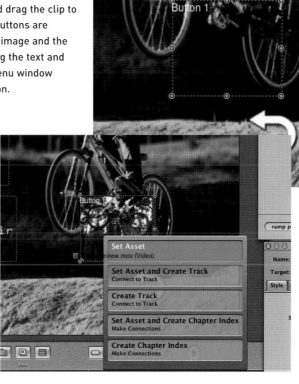

6 You'll need to re-size the movie preview button to make it hide the background still image icon. Use the interactive yellow guidelines to help you position the movie button accurately. You can re-size the button by dragging the corner handles. Unlike the first button you created with the rollover subpictures, this movie button is purely decorative. To stop the new button from getting in the way of the functional rollover button, Control + click on it and choose *Send to Back*.

7 Use the *Inspector* window to fine-tune the behaviour of the animated movie preview. You can adjust the starting point of the looped movie by dragging a slider to the desired frame. Test drive the menu using the *Simulate* option. It's important to make sure that the cosmetic movie preview button is layered behind the interactive rollover button so that it does not interfere with the navigation settings built into the rollover button.

Creating background movies

1 A background movie can comprise just a single clip from your main feature. However, you can make the menu more exciting by editing a montage of highlights from your movie in a non-linear editing package. This will excite the DVD user and make them want to see more. We used iMovie to create our montage of clips, but you could easily use Final Cut Express or Final Cut Pro. To edit your short background movie, create a new iMovie project, then import the media files from the original project that makes up your DVD's movie content.

2 Once your clips have been imported into the new project, you can edit them into a montage of the best bits. Restrict the duration of your DVD background movie to less than 30 seconds so that it can loop within the main DVD menu. Most menus loop to save on disc storage space. Use the yellow selection bars to select and crop the best parts of each clip. As the movie is short, keep it dynamic and punchy to make an impact when it is added to the DVD menu.

3 Once edited, the short movie montage can be visually stylized to become an animated menu background by using post-production digital effects in your editing package. iMovie 4 boasts a variety of video effects. Since our example stunt bike movie is dynamic and fast-paced, we applied a *Ghost Trail* filter to the clips. This allowed us to emphasize the speed of the bikes by adding a stylized *Motion Blur* effect. Experiment with other filters to find one suitable for the content of your DVD.

4 To make the short montage even more suitable as a stylized background menu movie, use a transition between each short shot in the sequence. Many non-linear editing packages offer a huge variety of wipes and fades. Many of these are less than subtle and can date your disc (especially the over-used *Lens Flare* filter!). Stick to the traditional *Cross Dissolve* to make the clips blend into each other in an elegant yet simple way. Finally, export your movie.

5 We can't simply replace our DVD's static chapter menu with our edited movie menu because the still background image contains all the button graphics. We need to create a mask to hide part of the movie so it doesn't eclipse the buttons on the main menu. In Photoshop, create a greyscale mask using the *Gradient* tool. The white sections will reveal the movie while the black sections will protect the background graphic so we can still see the buttons. Save it as a PSD, called 'Mask.PSD'.

6 In Studio Pro, draw a rectangular shaped button in the main menu window. Control + click within the button and select *Convert to Drop Zone* from the pop-up option. Import the background movie. Drag it into the *Drop Zone* to add it to the menu. Choose *Set Asset*. At this stage, the movie is hiding the buttons on the still background image. We need to apply the mask to hide part of the movie.

7 In the palette at the top-right of the Studio Pro interface, select *Shapes*. Click on *Custom* and *Import* the file Mask.psd. Click on the *Drop Zone* containing the background movie so that it displays in the *Inspector* window. In the *Drop Zone* palette, go to the *Shape* option and select Mask.PSD to apply it to the background movie. Click on the *Motion* icon to see the mask in action as it hides part of the background movie.

8 The *Drop Zone* containing the background movie will play in a loop. Thanks to the mask, you'll still be able to see the button icons and subpictures. You won't be able to see the animated movie previews though as the background movie has been added on top of them. Control + click on the background movie *Drop Zone* and choose *Send to Back*. This will ensure that the movie doesn't hide any of the other animated menu elements.

Designing with motion

As we have seen, the process of creating static DVD menus is fairly simple and uncomplicated if you stick within a few design limitations. A menu designer will usually work in Photoshop on a 72dpi canvas and design within NTSC safe areas, even when designing for PAL. Once navigation elements such as buttons are in place, a subpicture layer of simple bitmapped elements is added on top to provide the highlights on the final menu. All in all, a layered Photoshop TIFF file for a still menu will come to about 1MB.

But if you introduce motion, you take on a whole pile of extra design challenges and restrictions. First, consider the workload and rendering times – this is especially relevant if the whole disc is to contain motion menus. It is far more time consuming and difficult to correct a mistake with such menus than it is with menus that use a single, still image, because you have to re-render an entire animation. The type of material is also a factor – the DVD specification doesn't support small vector-based animations like Flash, so you have to use high-quality, full-motion video, often composited in applications like After Effects or Discreet Combustion. Another factor is size – just one simple menu page with five or six video buttons and audio can take up around 100MB. Multiply this for your submenus and extra feature screens and you will really begin to cut into the 4.37GB (realistic) capacity of the general DVD-R disc.

Below: *The designer of Morrissey's collection of eight promotional music videos, The Malady Lingers On, began by taking a suitable grab from each of the tracks. A 30-second sequence was edited together from these clips, with the options laid out on top of the video. When laying options over video in this way, a key factor to consider is legibility. Just as subtitles can be obscured by the background image (for example, white text on white), the same can happen on a DVD menu. To combat this on the Morrissey project, the background video was darkened, then the designer added a subtle Halftone filter effect in After Effects to create the look of footage as though filmed from a TV screen. The white text, with a little drop shadow added, stands out because there is no equivalent white in the background image to obscure it.*

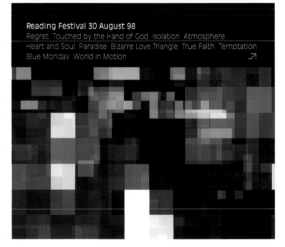

NewYork 81
Reading Festival 98
and in conversation

NewOrder 3 16

in conversation
subtitles English German All subtitles off ↗

Reading Festival 30 August 98
Regret Touched by the Hand of God Isolation Atmosphere
Heart and Soul Paradise Bizarre Love Triangle True Faith Temptation
Blue Monday World in Motion ↗

New York 18 November 81
ICB Dreams Never End Everything's Gone Green Truth
Senses Procession Ceremony Denial Temptation ↗

Left: *For this DVD of live material by the band New Order, the designer took footage from the concerts and used it as a basis for applying heavy pixelated effects. The Mosaic effect in After Effects created interesting abstract shapes and movement, while the bright colours against black captured the essence of a concert without being too obvious. As the background had a random feel to it and the colours were sharp and bright, it would have been difficult to ensure that the menu options were always visible, so areas of pure black were created on which to lay out the options and frame the motion.*

Design decisions

A key consideration in your design is whether you can use footage from the content of the disc or whether you have to create original material. You can, of course, use a mixture of the two. If you are using content from the programme, select a clip, or edit together a new sequence from a series of clips, that best highlight or capture the theme of the content.

Video formats and frame rates

If you are authoring your own video material for the DVD project, you'll already be familiar with the terms encoding and compression. This is how video intended for use on a DVD is converted to the compatible MPEG-2 format. This conversion involves a destructive form of compression, so you have to make sure that the source video is of the highest quality. The actual footage should also be shot as smoothly as possible. Lossy compression is not such a problem with the smaller size that you are likely to use for the video buttons, but it will affect the quality of full-screen motion backgrounds and transitions.

Still on the technical side, you also need to know in advance what format your DVD will play in. PAL has a frame rate of 25 frames per second (fps) as opposed to 30 fps for NTSC. If you're authoring for both formats, it makes sense to create your animations in PAL format first, then render the same animation at 30 fps for NTSC (after first resizing the dimensions as required) in After Effects or Combustion. After Effects is particularly useful here, as it has a *Frame Blending* feature that smoothes out the change to a higher frame rate. By creating additional frames, *Frame Blending* can stop unwanted frames from flashing during the menu loop.

Complex animation and motion

How the menu will loop, what animated elements you add, and whether or not you add audio, are all the factors that determine the length and complexity of the menu, as well as how much of the DVD's capacity it eats up. Make sure that the moving elements don't overwhelm the functionality or usability of the disc.

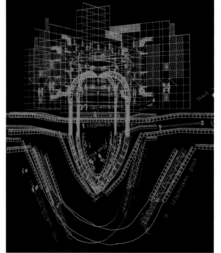

Right: U2 Go Home: Live from Slane Castle, Ireland. *This project had relatively little bonus content – just a documentary and some DVD-ROM material – but it required elaborate animated menus to engage the viewer and make the content attractive, while remaining easily accessible. The design team at Abbey Road Interactive (ARI) used fully animated looping menus with audio throughout.*

Above: *The footage had an orange hue applied to blend in with the colour scheme in a subtle way. Circular shapes emitting from either side of the stage were created to suggest sound waves in a graphic sense. These were turned into a looping animation, showing them growing in size then fading out. The 2D loop was tilted at an angle using the 3D space in After Effects to give the menu more depth. Everything was* designed to fit within the NTSC title safe area, although the DVD was intended for PAL viewing. It is better to design for the smaller of the two formats (NTSC) than create two versions, which can be very time consuming. The 16:9 aspect ratio allows much more information to fit onto a screen and, in this case, as much space as possible was used for a mere five options, which is an unusual luxury.

Above: *A stage plan blueprint was supplied and this was turned into a rotating animation. The level of detail in the plan gave added texture to the* menu without becoming too intricate. The 2D plan was duplicated and two planes were crossed in 3D to create a symbol rotating in the background.

Main menu
The concert had a specially developed stage in the shape of a heart, which was the emblem for the tour. Grabs were taken from the footage to form a basis for a main menu design. Infini-D was used to construct a 3D stage roof and a heart-shaped stage for the foreground. These were rendered in black and white and then colour was applied in After Effects. The menu options were laid out across the top of the stage and a video clip was positioned in the centre of the heart. Having a video of the concert playing in the main menu gives the viewer an idea of what to expect from the DVD.

Right: Following a decision to use the actual stage plan and ditch the 3D heart shape, the video space was replaced by four video projection screens at the top of the stage. Four video grabs of the band members were placed in the screens, so the options became four green text boxes and were moved under the four screens to give balance to the design and make them more visible. The fifth option was repositioned to the top-left of the stage roof. To make the options stand out even more, moving diagonal strips were added to the boxes to attract the eye during the menu loop. The subpicture was then set as a flat colour sitting on top of the diagonal lines of the selected option.

Left and below: It is a good idea to design for any eventuality, leaving space that could accommodate further options, but would not look suspiciously empty if none are added. In this case, the title of the disc was lengthened and another two options were added at a late stage. The final menu consists of multiple looped elements that can continue for as long as is necessary. The perspective of the stage and the 3D animations originating from the options mean the eye is always led into the centre, where the important information is placed. Even though the menu looks complex and contains many moving elements, it is quite clear where the options are. Ultimately, it is a dynamic, visually interesting, yet relevant menu.

Using animation

Here's another idea for creating background movies. Rather than simply editing a sequence together within Final Cut Pro (or your own preferred editing application), you can create an interesting look using a sequence of still frames, animated into a sequence. For the right subject matter, this can really help to build the atmosphere.

1 First, you need to create a sequence of still frames from an existing source. You could use a high-speed stills camera on a rapid shutter setting to capture the sense of movement on location. A more convenient method is to use your non-linear editing package to export a series of still frames from a video clip. Scrub forwards and backwards through the timeline to find your preferred stills. If you're using Final Cut Pro select *File → Export → **Using Quicktime Conversion*** and choose *Still Image* from the *Format* drop-down menu.

2 Import the exported stills into an image editor like Photoshop. It's possible that you may have annoying horizontal lines in the still images captured from video. This is due to the effects of interlacing, which becomes even more exaggerated in a still, so to clean up the image go to *Filter → Video → **De-Interlace***.

3 Using a series of stills to create the illusion of a moving sequence gives you greater control over the look of the sequence. You can take advantage of the fact that Photoshop has far more filters than any non-linear video editing software. Experiment with Photoshop's filters to get the desired look for your animated sequence. Once you've applied a filter to one layer, press Command + F to apply the same filter settings to the other frames.

4 After editing your exported stills in Photoshop, come full circle and bring them back into your editing package. You can then set their duration by double-clicking on each still. We set our example to 2 seconds per still and put a *Cross Dissolve* transition between them to create the illusion of movement. The shorter the duration of each still, the faster the movement will appear as you mix between the shots.

5 Now export your stills-based animated movie from your editing package and import it into your DVD project. You can set the animation as the background movie for an existing menu using the technique demonstrated on pages 108-111. This will let you mask out parts of the animated background. Alternatively, you can make the stylized background animation fill the entire menu interface and layer other components on top of the animation within Studio Pro.

6 Our first extreme biking sample chapter contained all the graphics and icons on a single Photoshop Layer. This limited us to a set design once we started working in Studio Pro. In this version, the background layer is an animated movie made up of stills, with buttons, layered on top. Inside the buttons we've added animated previews of the next three chapters. Instead of relying on text created in Photoshop, you can add text to buttons in Studio Pro.

7 To add text to a button in Studio Pro, click on the button and go to the *Inspector*. Type the relevant text into the *Text* field. Align it to the preferred side of the *Position* button in the *Text Formatting* section. You can fine-tune the text's position by using the offset channels. To edit the style of font, press Command + T to open the *Font* window.

8 You can make the text highlight and add a subpicture to the button entirely within Studio Pro, instead of creating the subpictures separately in Photoshop. In the *Text Formatting* section of the *Inspector*, check the *Include Text in Highlight* option. To create a subpicture, go to *Shapes* and choose *Simple Button*. Choose an *Opacity* setting. Now you can interact with the buttons while the background animation plays in a loop.

Stylized moving menu
This alternative chapter menu features an animated background movie made up of four filtered Photoshop stills. The overlaying buttons and subpictures were created within Studio Pro.

Creating transition effects

Transitions are motion clips that are used to smooth over the break between menus and submenus. The DVD-Video specification doesn't provide for built-in transitions on DVD players, so they need to be created in advance and treated just like any other piece of DVD content. The DVD player will pause as it cuts between motion menus, so transitions are a good way to ease the user through, and if done well, they are an attractive addition to the DVD.

Thematic transitions

Transitions range from simple wipes or dissolves to elaborate animations or even segments of the main feature. In any case, most professional transitions are designed to reflect the content of the disc. Accordingly, the menu system for the movie, *O Brother, Where art Thou?*, designed by ARI, uses a film wipe effect from the 1920s that enhances the period feel of the movie.

Above: *For any large DVD project, especially entertainment titles, transitions are essential and almost always expected. For Coldplay Live 2003, the visual look and feel of the transitions had to reflect the artwork and the menu design,* complementing them at every step. The fragile and delicate look of the artwork was reflected in particle transition animations that seemed to blow the menu away in a gust of wind, suggesting a certain lightness of touch. They also give you a sense of traveling around within the disc and make the experience more interactive and 'journey' based.

The nature of the artwork meant that animating it had to be a subtle process. Particle Systems II *in After Effects was used to create tiny polygons and tetrahedrons that would swarm across the screen in random patterns. They were masked on to 2D wireframe artwork and gently blended in to appear as though they were following the lines of the figure.*

Above: *For the transitions between chapters and the main menu on O Brother, Where Art Thou?, the designer created an oval window in which to play selected clips* from the movie. The screens were designed to look like elaborate pages from a book, and coloured according to the menu they were going to or from. These allowed easy movement out of the main menu, which took the form of simple cuts rather than any complicated animation. All the clips selected are humorous, and short enough to have an impact over a few seconds. As the clip comes to an end, there is a diagonal wipe to the next menu, which is also a characteristic filmic device from the period.

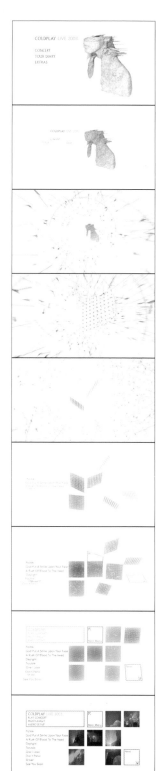

Left: *For the transitions, the Cylinder Perspective effect in After Effects was used to wrap the 2D animation around and create a depth to the particles. In the transition between the Main Menu and Setlist 1, the particles are fashioned into a tunnel and the viewer is propelled backward through it as the main menu zooms away.*

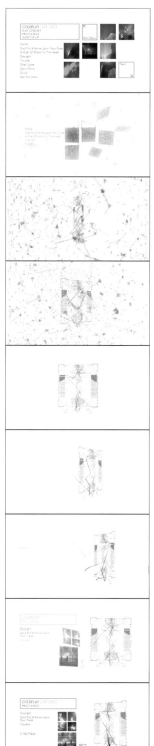

Left: *On the main menu, the particles self-generate every few seconds then fade away to repeat the cycle. For the transitions between Main Menu to Extras and between the Setlist 1 screen to the Multiangle menu, the effect resembles a cyclone of particles that picks up the menu and ends with a new menu falling in its place.*

Complex transitions

No matter how artistic or complex you want to be with transitions, remember that they take both time and effort to get right and, most importantly, they must aid and not detract from the user experience. The time taken for transitions is all-important. You want them to be just long enough to create something visually interesting and to introduce the new menu, but brief enough so as not to become repetitive and irritating. Generally speaking, transitions should be no longer than 3–5 seconds, much shorter if possible.

If you are taking a user from one moving menu to another you also have to make sure that the transition is smooth and does not jar with the menu loop. The norm is to begin the transition with the last frame of the outgoing menu and end it with the first frame of the new menu. Giving the transitions a consistent look, sense of movement, and timing helps to gel the interfaces together and give the user a smoother experience. It would become irritating, for example, if one transition was short but the following one very long.

Above: *The U2* Go Home *concert DVD contains several menu transitions of varying complexity. One of these is the sequence that evolves from the main menu to the track selection menu. For this transition, the 3D stage elements animate off the screen while the general background cross-fades to that of the new Tracks menu. The start frame has to* feature something that will not jump abruptly when selected from the main menu, so these transitions are made via trigger animations, which allow the user to trigger the transition at any point within a 40-second loop. A lot is happening at any moment within that time frame, so a flash frame was added in the form of the options— the only element that never changes from menu to menu. The moving background is flashed out for a few frames so that any discontinuity between different looped elements is obscured and, to the viewer's eye, everything is running smoothly. This happens at the beginning and end of every menu loop, depending on the variable durations of the individual looped elements. Rather than trying to get everything to start and end looping simultaneously, the designer set the background to flash out for a few frames, rising to white at the end and fading down from white at the beginning. Any inconsistencies go unnoticed and the viewer can close the menu at any frame they desire.

Right: *For the main menu to Tracks Menu sequence, 3D elements were introduced to sit on the new menu, such as a wireframe mesh and a 3D animated heart. The images here show the animated models as well as the compositing process in After Effects as an illustration of how* the layers of the sequence were built up. Throughout the loop of the tracks, a pixel animation plays out on the wireframe mesh grid. This was achieved by switching on the relevant grid squares on their layers for each frame. These frames then build into an animation over time.

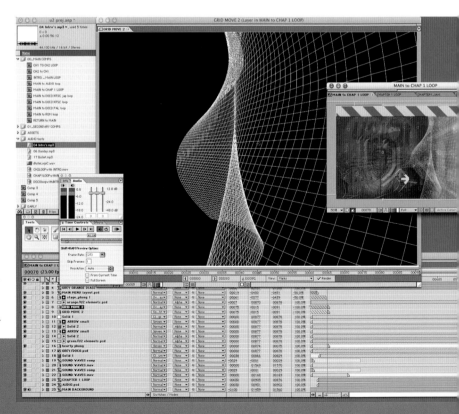

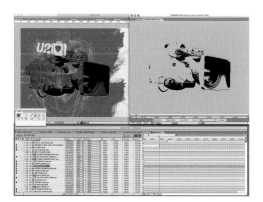
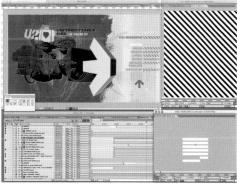
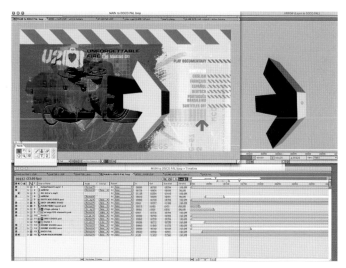

Left: *Another transition on the U2 Go Home disc is the sequence that carries the viewer from the main menu to the Documentary. This was achieved using the same process as the Menu to Tracks transition. The individual elements were brought together and composited in After Effects. The screen grabs show the animated diagonal lines for the options that can be seen through a mask that sits next to the text. The grabs also show how a photo of a video camera treated in Photoshop and an arrow created in Infini-D are composited onto the menu, and the colours inverted to work better with the menu design.*

Intro transitions

Another type of transition is the first play or intro transition. This is a useful device as it introduces the viewer to the themes and tone of the DVD. A more elaborate intro generally indicates that the menu, and content, will be an interesting and interactive experience. Or it can be the only animated section of the disc, used to pad out an otherwise empty interface. The intro transition will only play once–when the viewer inserts the DVD.

Above: *These images show the animated sequence leading into the main menu, designed by ARI, for the U2 Go Home DVD. The designer wanted to use this sequence to establish the band members and the location. Four sections of footage of each member were colour treated and freeze-framed and then composited together* *with an animation introducing pieces of the U2 logo. The DVD title was established over a rotating 3D map of the Slane Castle site and all the elements were combined in After Effects with audio from the U2 song 'Bullet the Blue Sky'.*

As the first play cycle is not repeated, it is acceptable to have quite long sequences. Accordingly, the intro *transition was allowed to be between 15 to 20 seconds. To continue the theme, it leads smoothly into the main menu loop, which continues with the same piece of audio for another 30 to 40 seconds–the average length of a menu loop.*

Right: *As the intro transition for a series of DVDs of the popular* Thunderbirds *series, the designer created a 3D model of Thunderbird 1 and set the rocket to fly out towards the viewer in an exciting opening animation, complete with smoke, falling 3D debris, and rocket blast effects. A hangar interior was created using grabs from the show, the rocket was built in Amapi, textures were created in Photoshop, and the model was brought into Infini-D for animating and rendering. All elements were brought into After Effects to composite them with the menu and then particle smoke and rocket blast effects were added, all rendered with* Particle Systems 2.

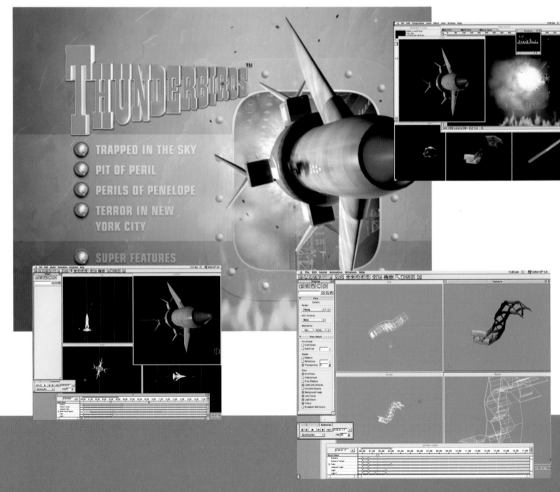

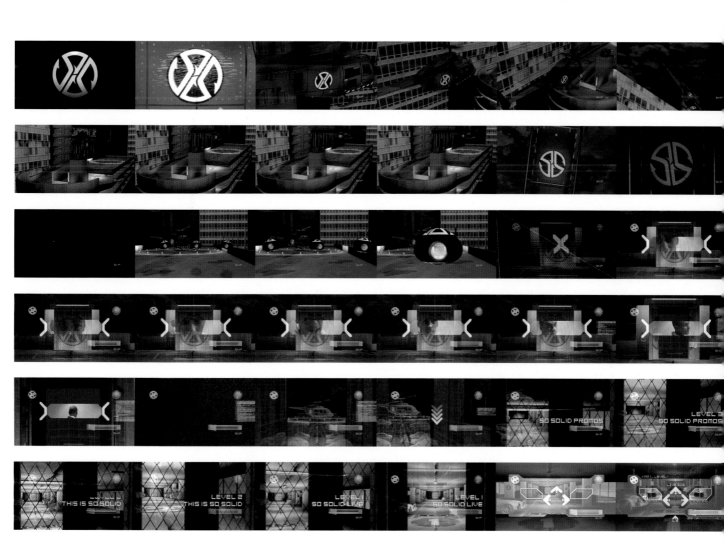

Above: So Solid Crew DVD
Record label Independiente commissioned ARI to create an interactive extravaganza for the So Solid Crew DVD, complete with a 3D visual landscape for the menu system. A complex animated intro sequence was devised to introduce the parking ramp setting for the menu, the characters, and the various levels and their contents before the user started. However, the sequence was fairly long, even for an intro transition, so a skip option was implemented in the design.

Making a moving menu
Creating an introduction sequence

Over the next few pages, we'll work through the process of creating a menu for a short science-fiction movie – *They Came for a Day*. It's important to become familiar with the look and feel of the DVD's content so that you can create a menu that complements the content. *They Came for a Day* is an affectionate homage to the alien invasion movies that dominated the cinema of the 50s and 60s. Genre movies like this have a strong visual style and suggest a deliberately tawdry, B-movie style menu.

We created our introduction sequence for *They Came for a Day* using Premiere and After Effects. The former was used to digitize the edited footage into the computer. We then looked through the footage and used the *Razor Blade* tool to isolate clips that might be appropriate in the intro sequence. We moved these clips onto a separate video channel then double-clicked on them to export them as QuickTime movies. We could have created the montage entirely in Premiere using transitions to dissolve from one clip to the next, but After Effects provides more visual effects that can help us stylize the introductory montage. Be aware that After Effects is not designed as an editing package. It is a post-production package that enables you to manipulate shots digitally, which will then be incorporated back into a movie using a non-linear editing package like Premiere. However, because our introduction sequence is short, we can get away with creating it entirely within After Effects.

Left: *Use an editing package like Adobe Premiere to select and export short clips to After Effects so that digital effects can be added to them.*

Creating an introduction sequence

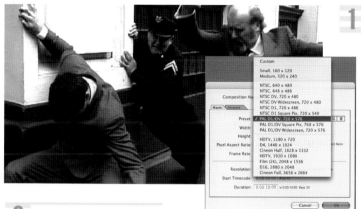

1 When using Premiere to choose clips from your DVD's feature movie to add to the introduction montage, select shots that have movement in them to add some excitement and energy to the sequence. Decide whether you are going to cut the shots to music, or keep any dialogue audible. For our B-movie intro sequence, we avoided using any clips with the actors talking, and compiled a short series of action clips with music playing in the background. This way, our intro sequence has a flavour of the movie but doesn't give away any plot details.

2 Once you've selected the short clips that you want to feature in your menu's introduction sequence, you'll need to import them into After Effects. Go to *File → New Composition*. Make sure that you set the new composition to the appropriate settings for your DVD's content. As we were working on a UK disc, we chose the European PAL format, which our movie was shot in. This makes our movie's size 720 pixels wide by 576 pixels high at 72 dpi.

3 Import the clips into After Effects by selecting *File → Import → Multiple Files*. Hold down the Shift key and select the short movie clips you exported from Premiere. They will appear in the main After Effects Project window. Drag the first clip in the sequence to the *Timeline*. Click on the little triangle by the clip to view its *Transform* options. With the Time slider set to the first frame, click on the *Keyframe* icon (the little clock) to set a key. Reduce the *Opacity* to 0%. *Advance* forward a few frames and set the *Opacity* to 100%. This will cause the image to fade in from black.

4 We could simply dissolve between the shots in our montage, but that's something we could do in Premiere. After Effects allows more creative control when it comes to adding visual effects to footage. To emphasize the sci-fi genre of the DVD, we'll cause a lens flare to occur between each clip, hiding one shot and revealing the next. This transition will reference nicely with 50s sci-fi movies and their associated paraphernalia, like ray guns and A-bombs. Select the first clip and go to *Effect → Render → Lens Flare*.

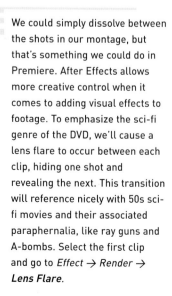

RAM

When you apply filters to your footage in After Effects, it's helpful to see the effect of the filters in real time. To do this, right-click in the *Timeline* and choose *Preview › RAM Preview* from the pop-up context menu. After Effects will then render as much of the sequence as it can fit into your computer's RAM to show you the filters in action.

5 When you add a visual effect, a new *Effects* label appears in the *Timeline*. Open it up to see the editable *Lens Flare* attributes. When you add a *Lens Flare* to the shot it defaults to a *50-300mm Zoom* lens placed in the centre of the frame. We changed it to a *105mm Prime* lens to reduce the colour of the flare so that it was more in keeping with our monochrome footage. After Effects enables you to animate the position of the flare and keyframe its intensity. Select the *Flare Center* channel and position the source of the flare where required.

6 Our footage shows a character lifting an alien blob into shot, so we placed the *Flare Center* over the blob and set two keyframes to make the *Flare Center* move into shot as the blob is lifted up by one of the characters. We keyed the *Flare Brightness* channel so that the flare would start at 0% and flare up to 137%. As the flare fills the screen, everything turns to white. This disguises the edit point where we can cut to the next shot in the montage.

7 To make the transition from the first shot to the second work effectively, we added a *Lens Flare* effect, but keyframed the *Flare Brightness* to start at 215% so that the first few frames of the second shot would be pure white. We then keyframed the flare to reduce to 0% to reveal the next shot. As the end of the first shot and the beginning of the second are burned out by the flare, the cut between the two shots is disguised and more fluid. We also keyframed the *Flare Center* to track the movement of the character's gun to give the transition more movement.

8 We added more rapid *Lens Flare* effect transitions between each shot in the DVD's introduction sequence. Our final shot ends with a hubcap-style flying saucer heading toward the moon. We chose to use this shot against a star field as the background for our main menu. As well as being fun in a 50s-style sci-fi way, it leaves plenty of space to add text.

Preparing Photoshop graphics

1 When you jump between video and graphic packages, you
need to be aware that a computer monitor and a TV screen
use different shaped pixels. This may not seem significant,
but it can lead to fundamental problems with your menu if not
taken into account. The computer monitor's pixels are square;
TV screens use non-square pixels. When you export an image
created in Photoshop to a video editing package, it will
become scaled to fit the non-square pixels of the TV screen.
This means your computer-created menus could stretch out
of shape when displayed on TV.

TIP
Aspect ratio
Once you've created
a file using the TV
screen presets, you
can see what the
image looks like
without being
scaled by going to
the main *View* menu
and turning off
*Pixel Aspect Ratio
Correction*.

2 As our moon image was sourced from video, it looked
elliptical when displayed in Photoshop. To get around the
difference between TV and PC monitor pixels, we had to
create a new file in Photoshop. Go to *File → New* and select a
PAL or NTSC preset. This will make Photoshop scale the new
file so that what you see on the monitor will be displayed
accurately on a TV screen. We pasted our shot of the moon
into the Photoshop preset PAL TV file and used the *Transform*
tool to scale it to fit. The two moon images look different in
size, but both are 720 x 576 pixels in resolution. The apparent
difference is caused by Photoshop scaling the lower image to
compensate for video's non-square pixels.

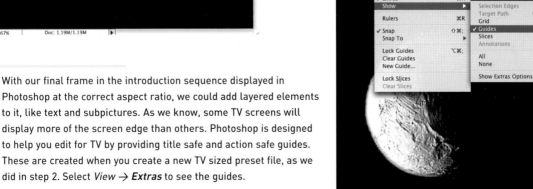

3 With our final frame in the introduction sequence displayed in
Photoshop at the correct aspect ratio, we could add layered elements
to it, like text and subpictures. As we know, some TV screens will
display more of the screen edge than others. Photoshop is designed
to help you edit for TV by providing title safe and action safe guides.
These are created when you create a new TV sized preset file, as we
did in step 2. Select *View → Extras* to see the guides.

4 All TVs are slightly different. Some will have screens that are aligned slightly left, others slightly to the right. The action safe guide is the outer marker. It isn't so crucial if some of the menu graphics like the star field disappear at the edge of the screen. But keep all your buttons within the inner title safe guide. It would be a major disaster for your menu if you created a button that was just off the edge of the user's TV screen.

5 We set out to make our sci-fi DVD's menu match the look and style of the disc's feature. To this end, we made sure that the font used on the main menu matched the font used in the opening titles of the movie. Mismatching fonts stop a disc's assets from mixing smoothly together. So, if you have a movie menu to create, it's always worth finding out what fonts are used in the main title sequence.

6 We chose the font Impact, which comes with Photoshop so there was no need to make an extra purchase. If you do need to shop around for third-party fonts, you can check out a variety of websites that enable you to download copyright-free fonts. Bear in mind that when designing for TV, your menu text should be large and bold. Anti-alias your font to avoid buzzing and line fighting. To make our white font stand out against the white moon, we decided to copy the movie's caption style by adding a black line around the outline of the font.

7 To create an outline around a font, you first have to rasterize the text. This means it will become a solid bitmap image instead of an editable text layer. But before you rasterize, double-check that the spelling is correct. There are some horror stories out there concerning designers who delivered their menus with typing errors, rendering the whole menu useless and causing expensive delays and unhappy clients. Don't rely on the authoring stage to sort out problems like spelling errors. Check now.

8 To add an outline to the text, rasterize it by right-clicking (Control-clicking on a Mac) to the right of the text layer's thumbnail in the *Layers* palette. Then go to *Edit → Stroke*. Select the colour for the text's outline, and choose an appropriate pixel size. Be careful not to make the stroke too small, as horizontal stroke lines on the text will buzz if the line only appears on one field of the TV screen.

Adding layered elements in Photoshop

1 Now let's add some menu buttons, using the techniques used on the previous page. Make sure that the buttons are within the title safe area. You don't need to *Stroke* these buttons as their final position is against the black space background. Placing the buttons on separate layers will allow us to animate them in After Effects to make them fly into the scene to assume their final positions. To keep them in the style of 50s sci-fi, we added exclamation marks after each button.

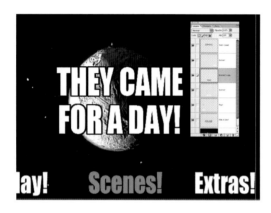

2 The next step is to create a subpicture that will indicate which button the user has selected. This is also an opportunity to add a hint of colour to the menu. Right-click on the text layer thumbnail and choose *Select Layer Transparency* from the pop-up menu. Create a new layer and fill it with green. Green is a colour often associated with aliens and bug-eyed monsters. We reduced the *Opacity* of the subpicture layer to 50%.

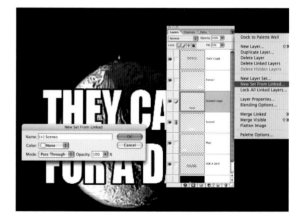

3 Our menu is going to be taken into After Effects so that motion can be added. The subpictures need to be in a format that will be recognized by Adobe Encore, otherwise they will not be visible when we come to author the menu. Select the text and link it to its subpicture by clicking the chain icon. Then go to the pop-up menu at the top-right of the *Layers* palette and choose *New Set From Linked*. Label the set '(+) Scenes.' The (+) sign tells Encore that this layer set is a button.

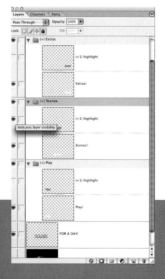

4 You also need to label the layers within the button set to tell Encore which layer is a subpicture and what highlight state it represents (selected or activated, for example). Our green text will indicate to the menu user that a button is selected. Label it '(=1) highlight'. If we decide to add an activated highlight later, we can call that '(=2) highlight'. The advantage in working between Photoshop, After Effects, and Encore is that we can jump back and forth between each package to make menu changes at any stage of the project. Once the button sets have been created, turn off the subpicture highlights to make them invisible.

Adding motion in After Effects

1 Open your intro movie After Effects project. Import the layered main menu Photoshop document into After Effects. Go to *File → Import → File*. In the *Import File* dialog box, select your PSD file and choose to *Import it as a Composition*. This will give you a folder in the After Effects assets window containing all the layers from your Photoshop document. It also creates a new After Effects composition displaying all the layered text elements.

2 We're going to create an animation where the various elements that make up the main menu fly in to take up their final menu positions. We'll start with the words 'They Came'. Open up that layer in the *Timeline* to see its transform options. Drag the time indicator to the end of the *Timeline* and set keyframes for the *Anchor Point*, *Position*, and *Scale* channels. It is important that the finished position of the text matches exactly the position of the text on the still menu (otherwise there will be a jump in the menu's components and the subpictures may misalign).

3 Drag the time indicator back to frame 1. Now you can animate the position and scale values of the layer, safe in the knowledge that whatever you do with the text, it will end up in the desired position at the end of the sequence. We scaled down the 'They Came' text layer and positioned it at the centre of the moon. We then set a new keyframe with the *Scale* channel set at 0. This caused the text to fly in from the centre of the screen and finish in exactly the right position, thanks to the end keyframe.

4 We keyed the 'For a Day!' text to zoom in in the same way. By dragging the keyframes around, we offset 'For a Day!' so that it zoomed into view slightly behind the first line of text. This added a sense of depth and variety to the animated text layers. We animated the button text using the same technique. The 'Play!' button slides in from the left. The 'Scenes!' button pops up from below the screen and the 'Extras!' button flies in from screen right. We dragged the keyframe icons around to offset the buttons to make them fly in at slightly different times. We made them arrive after the title had finished zooming in.

Adding 3D elements

On the previous spread, we created motion effects for the end of the menu introduction sequence, whereby the text and button elements fly in to adopt their final positions in the menu. Now let's create a motion menu to give the main DVD menu some movement. The user will have something animated to watch while they make their menu choice. To run with the sci-fi theme, we'll add an animated flying saucer and make it fly around the scene. The UFO can also be used to create some animated transition movies.

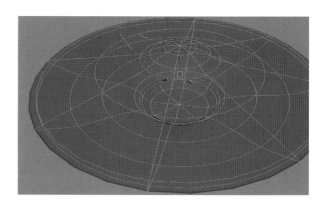

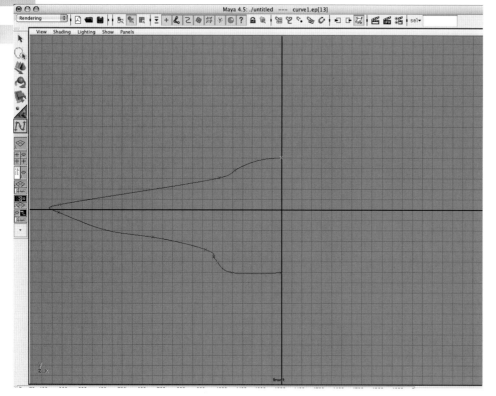

1 3D modelling packages are another useful tool for the DVD menu designer. But be warned – they take time and commitment to master. Some menus are created entirely in 3D and give the impression that the menu user is moving from room to room to select different menu options. You need to decide whether your menu really needs a 3D component. Will it help the user find content or would it function only as a gimmick? We decided to use Maya, a high-end 3D modelling package to create an animation of a flying saucer to add to our motion menu.

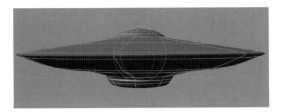

2 Virtually all 3D packages allow you to create a flying saucer using the same technique. Go to a side view and choose a *Curve* tool to draw the profile of a UFO. It works in a similar way to Photoshop's *Pen* tool in that you place anchor points to create a curve. The 3D package will then let you create a solid looking shape by revolving the curve through 360 degrees. Apply a texture to the shape to create a saucer with a metallic look.

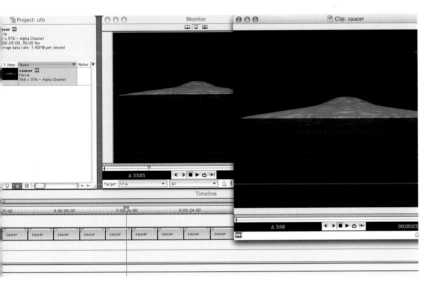

3 Make sure the saucer is close enough to the camera. You can scale it down in After Effects, but you can't scale it up beyond 100% without losing quality. If in doubt, render it to fill the frame. But first, decide what the saucer is going to do. Rendering the animation in 3D takes a great deal of time, so keyframe the model to fully rotate once through 359 degrees. The plan is to loop the saucer movie in Premiere to extend it – if you had the saucer rotating at a full 360 degrees, there would be a slight stutter at the end of each loop.

4 When rendering your 3D movie in Premiere to extend it, make sure that you preserve its alpha channel information. If you don't, it won't be easy to make the areas outside the saucer transparent when you import the file into After Effects. Go to the main Premiere menu bar and choose *Project → Project Settings → Video*. Set the *Compressor* to *Animation*. Set the *Depth* to *Millions +*. The + sign means that any alpha channel information will be preserved.

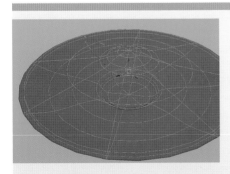

TIP
Alpha channels
Make sure your 3D software allows you to render out an alpha channel with your animation. This will allow you to add it to the main menu After Effects and have the area outside of the saucer totally transparent so that it overlays seamlessly onto the 2D menu elements.

5 Once you've turned your short 3D animation into a longer looping sequence in Premiere (or any other editing application that supports alpha channels), go back to your After Effects project and choose *Composition → **New Composition***. Label the new composition Motion Menu. Go to *File → **Import*** to bring in the looped rotating UFO movie. As you want to preserve its alpha channel, choose the S*traight – Unmatted* option from the *Interpret Footage* dialog.

6 Drag the folder containing the layered menu components from the project assets window onto the new composition's *Timeline*. Notice that each component has a layer of its own. Drag the saucer movie to the *Timeline* and place it on a layer below the text buttons. It is important that the saucer doesn't fly above the text, as this would interfere with the user's access to the buttons. As the alpha channel has been preserved, the saucer overlays the menu without you having to key out the file's black background.

7 Experiment with your 3D animated component by using the *Move* tool to change its position. Thanks to its support for layers, After Effects behaves just like Photoshop and lets the saucer fly over the background text but underneath the buttons. You can swap the layer order of the composition's components to make the saucer fly behind the title text if you want, simply by dragging the stacked layers labels around in the *Timeline*. Next, we'll keyframe the UFO to fly in and out of the shot, as well as towards the camera.

8 We're going to have the saucer buzz in and out of the menu to add motion to it. First we have to decide how long our menu is going to play before it loops. If we make it too short, there is a danger that the user will become irritated by the loop temporarily stopping them from accessing the buttons. Looping menu music can also be irritating. We decided to make our menu loop for 30 seconds, which gives us long enough for the UFO to perform a variety of different moves. Extend the timeline duration by typing in a higher value in the *Composition Settings* window. You can access this by clicking on the arrow at the top-right of the *Timeline*.

9 When the intro sequence has finished playing and the text has finished zooming in, we want the cut from the animated intro sequence to the main menu to be smooth and unnoticeable. This means the 3D saucer has to be out of shot to start with, otherwise it will appear on the menu as a jarring jump cut. Zoom out to see the edges around the menu. Enlarge the main window so you can see the edges of the menu screen. Select the *Move* tool and drag the saucer onto the grey work area to hide it.

10 Scale the UFO down to about half size. Place its layer underneath the 'They Came for a Day!' text layer. Open the UFO layer's *Transform* option and add a keyframe to the *Anchor Point*, *Position*, *Scale* and *Rotation* channels. Advance the *Time* slider to frame 10 and drag the saucer to the other side of the screen so that it flies behind the main title and exits screen right. Set new keyframes for the end of the move. To make the saucer oscillate like the deliberately poor special effect in the feature, keyframe its *Rotation* channel to add a hint of wobble.

11 To make the UFO fly above the title text but behind Play! Scenes!, and Extras!, drag the original movie from the Project assets window onto the *Timeline*. Place this on a layer above the title text but below the button text and keyframe it to fly from screen left to screen right. You could create a fleet of flying saucers from one movie using this technique. As our DVD is a homage to low-budget sci-fi movies, we limited ourselves to one UFO flying in and out of the menu.

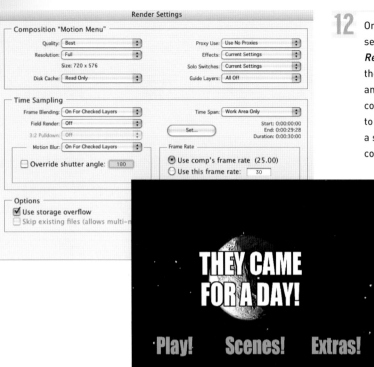

12 Once you've finished creating animated movies for the introduction sequence and the DVD's motion menu, go to *Composition → **Add to Render Queue**. Make sure that you're going to render movies that are the same size and resolution as your Photoshop components to avoid any unwanted changes in size once you start to combine all the components together in Encore. As our sci-fi DVD movie is designed to be PAL compatible, we set our output to 720 by 576 pixels. Choose a sensible name for each composition and render them out as complete movies.

13 Open Encore and create a new project. Make sure you choose the same PAL or NTSC settings you used to create your still and moving menu assets in Photoshop, Premiere, and After Effects. Right-click in the *Project* tab and choose *Import as Menu* from the pop-up menu. Select the multi-layered Photoshop document that contains the menu buttons, background, and subpictures. Check that the subpictures display correctly by clicking on the *Show Selected Highlight* button at the bottom of the main menu window. In our example, the buttons turn green. Encore recognizes the subpicture layers due to the (=) sign we labelled them with.

14 We don't actually need much of the layered Photoshop document, as we will replace most of it with the animated menu sequence we created in After Effects. The only components we need to keep are the subpictures, so use the *Layers* palette to turn off all the button and background elements. Then go to the project window, right-click and choose *Import as Asset*. Bring in the animated background sequence that was created in After Effects. Encore will automatically transcode into MPEG-2 to make the footage suitable for DVD.

15 It's a simple matter to add the animated background movie to the main menu. Select the main menu in the *Project* window and open the *Properties* tab. Next to the *Video* channel is a little circular icon. This indicates that you can use a pick whip to link assets to that channel. To see the pick whip in action, click and drag from the circular icon next to the *Video* channel. A line appears as you drag. Drag the line to the After Effects video clip in the *Projects* window. This tells Encore to place the movie in the menu's background.

Linking up your menu assets in Encore

16 Test the menu to make sure that the movie plays and that the subpictures are correctly aligned with the text on the background movie. They should match perfectly, as you created the moving menu by using the same layered Photoshop file as a template. This demonstrates the advantages of using After Effects, Photoshop, and Encore together. Go to *File Preview* to bring up a DVD preview window. This will mimic the behaviour of the DVD user's remote so you can test-drive the menu to make sure that the subpictures appear.

17 We need to decide what happens when the main menu has finished playing. Odds are you'll want the menu to loop forever until a menu button has been selected, so you can choose that option from the Loop # channel in the menu's *Properties* window. You could decide that the menu will loop for a certain number of times and then begin playing the movie. All of these options are available to you in the *Properties* tab.

18 Now that we know that our motion menu and the subpictures work as designed, we can start to link up our menu to be more interactive. We want the introductory montage clip to play when the DVD is first put into the player to lead us to the main menu. We edited the clip montage and the text zoom movie together using Premiere and imported them as an asset into Encore. Create a new timeline by going to *Timeline → New Timeline*. Drag the introduction clip into the new timeline and label it 'Intro Movie Timeline'. To get this clip to play before the main menu appears, right-click on the intro movie timeline in the *Project* window and choose *Set As First Play*.

19 Once the introduction clip has played, we need to tell Encore what happens next. This package takes nothing for granted. Select the *Intro Movie* timeline in the *Projects* tab so that it shows in the *Properties* box. Go to the *End Action* channel and use the pick whip to make a link from the *End Action* option to the main menu asset in the *Properties* window. This will cause the main menu to appear once the introduction sequence has played. The main menu will then loop until a button has been selected. Our menu's front end is now complete and mixes the motion clips and the layered Photoshop file together.

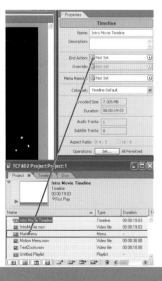

Creating menu transitions in After Effects

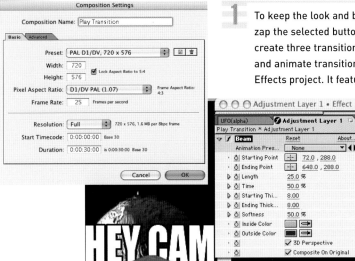

1 To keep the look and behaviour of the menu consistent, we decided to make the flying saucer zap the selected button with a laser and knock it out of the menu. This meant we needed to create three transitional movies—one for each button in the main menu. We can easily create and animate transition movies to add to our Encore project by adapting the existing After Effects project. It features all the components we need to create animated transitions.

2 First we opened the After Effects project used to create the background motion menu, and then created a new composition. We called it *Play Transition*. We added the layered Photoshop file containing the text and background elements. We also added the UFO movie and scaled it to rest over the main title. To add a laser beam, we need to create a new layer for it to render on. Right-click (Control-click on a Mac) in the *Timeline* and choose *New Adjustment Layer*. Select the layer in the *Timeline* and choose *Effect → Render → Beam*. To make the beam overlay on the image, select *Composite on Original* in the adjustment layer's *Effects* channel.

3 To make the laser beam fly from the saucer to the Play! button, select the start and end points in the *Effects* channel. Place the time indicator at the position in the *Timeline* where you want the beam to start firing from. Leave a couple of seconds at the start of the sequence before the laser fires. Key the *Time* channel at 0% to place the beam at the starting point. Advance the time indicator a second or so and key the beam's *Time* channel at 100%. The laser will fly from the saucer to the text. Key the text to fade away or fly out of shot at this event.

4 Create another two transitional movies of the saucer shooting the Scenes! and Extras! buttons. As it's impossible to tell when in the main menu sequence the user will press a button, we need to disguise the fact that the saucer will jump from one part of the screen in the main menu sequence to the centre part of the screen in the transition movie. Add a lens flare effect to the beginning of each transition movie to disguise the change in position of the animated elements. This is a common trick used by DVD menu designers to hide discrepancies in the position of animated elements during transitional sequences.

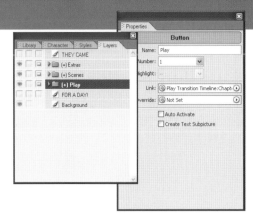

5 Once you've made your short transition movies in a package like Premiere or After Effects, import the movies into the *Project* window in Encore. We also digitized the main sci-fi feature into our PC using Premiere's *Capture* option. Import the main movie into Encore, too, plus any other assets like submenu graphics and "making of" features. You can then use Encore to start linking the different assets together to make the DVD menu interactive.

6 Let's set up the Play! button to become interactive. You need to make sure that when it is clicked, the menu plays the correct transition movie before playing the main feature. Before you set up the Play! button, create a new *Timeline* and add the main feature movie to it. Label the *Timeline* "Main Movie Timeline". Create another *Timeline* and add the Play Transition movie to that. Label it accordingly. Select the Play! button on the main menu by using the *Selection* tool. Its properties will appear in the *Properties* window.

7 Once the Play! button's properties are visible, use the pick whip to link the Play! button to the Play transition timeline. Then select the Play Transition timeline to see its properties. Use the pick whip to link the *End Action* property to the Main Movie *Timeline*. Once your buttons and movies have been linked together, hit Alt + Control + Space to preview the menu and take it for a test run. The introduction movie should play, the text zoom in, and the main menu should loop. Hitting the Play! button will cause the screen to flare up as the menu cuts to a transition. The saucer will then zap the Play! button and the main feature will play.

8 Continue using the pick whip to link up all of your assets. Then get a friend who is unfamiliar with the menu to take it for a test drive. They may spot problems that you haven't. Some DVD players clip transitions, so make sure you have at least eight frames run in at the start of the transition that aren't crucial. Edit any sound in a transition to fade up over the first few frames to avoid sound clipping. Go to *Window → Disc* to get a visual preview of how much DVD storage capacity your assets are taking. When you're happy with the menu, go to *File → Build DVD → Make DVD Disc*.

Triggered elements

The DVD format is highly interactive due to its ability to provide non-linear access to disc content. Although there are some restrictions, you can easily add interest to your menu with interactive elements. When the user can see their actions having some effect, it gives them a satisfying sense of feedback.

Buttons and subpictures

As we have seen, menu transitions are essentially triggered elements – the result of selecting a button. The buttons themselves can be animated, but the button subpicture overlay cannot be. Subpictures are merely markers that let the user know what option they have selected from a menu. As the subpicture is a static layer above the video and cannot be animated, the options generally have to remain in situ on the menu below – if your options moved across screen, the buttons would not relate to anything. To create an animated effect, therefore, buttons have to be animated prior to DVD authoring and composited onto the video background. These restrictions make DVD seem less interactive than other interface designs, such as a rich media Flash website, which allows for more innovation and functionality. However, a good designer can learn to work with these restrictions and make them appear integral to the menu design rather than just a low-tech layer of hard-edged graphics.

Right: *When the subpictures are switched on in the menu for the Thunderbirds series, each colour is allocated black at three varying opacities to mimic anti-aliasing, while all the underlying red frames have their colour subdued except the one that is chosen.*

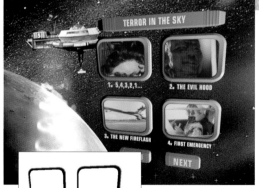

Left: *In the first screen, the monitor frames have bright red frames, indicating the normal, untriggered state.*

Left: *In this case, the subpictures do the opposite of what they normally do. Instead of acting as button highlights when activated, the subpictures were programmed to remain on throughout the menu loop, with the exception of the one chosen by the viewer.*

Cause and effect

Designers can also use the menu system itself to create surprise elements that come into play when the user presses an element of the menu or uses the direction buttons of the remote after selecting a graphic. These hidden extras, or 'Easter eggs', can be fiendishly disguised and often very hard to find on a complex menu screen if the user doesn't know where to look.

Right: *The more hidden the extra content is, the more intent a user can be to find it, which maintains excitement in the DVD. For the* Best of Bowie *DVD release, ARI even concealed an 'Easter egg' within a hidden extra. Once a certain hidden video is discovered and played, the viewer is given the chance to notice a subpicture positioned over a television during a scene. If this is selected at the right time, they are treated to a further alternative version of the video. To guide the fans that wished to discover these hidden extras, clues were posted on the official Bowie website.*

Right: *The DVD for* Best of Bowie *has many hidden features. On the Tracks menu on the first disc, the subpictures are highlighted in red and orange. Selecting right on your remote control at 'Blue Jean' brings up a parenthesis shape. If you then select this with the remote, you trigger a transition to an alternative version of that track. Navigating further right allows the user to select one of the picture boxes, which also plays a hidden video.*

Below: *This screen from the So Solid Crew DVD shows a hidden subpicture. The four people sitting in cars are selectable subpictures, but when the user arrives, there is nothing on the menu to indicate that they are there. The viewer has to be adventurous to find them and trigger the interaction.*

Above: *A clever designer can also bring interaction to the menu's main content. A game for the Creative Review magazine DVD was devised around the theme of time. It involved an animated circular puzzle containing five pieces. At each of the five stages, the user has to use the remote to select the right puzzle piece from a choice of three in an ever-decreasing amount of time. The correct piece triggers the next successive animation while the wrong piece ends the game and returns the user to the menu.*

Using sound and music in menus

Up until now, we have been concerned with design and usability rules for video and graphics, but DVD also offers the option of adding audio to your menus. The large capacity of the disc means that multiple tracks of audio can be laid down – soundtracks, alternate commentaries, music selections, and foreign language dialogue. As well as providing your viewer with a means to select the various audio tracks, the menu system will typically contain some sound of its own.

Below: *Consumer DVD players use audio based on the PCM, DTS, or the Dolby Digital AC-3 file formats. You can use the DVD menu to offer the user the option to choose whatever format their home entertainment system can handle and give them a taste of the effects.*

The use of audio can really bring a menu system to life and is standard on most professional DVDs. The menu of *U2 Go Home* features surround-sound audio of the song 'Bullet the Blue Sky', which makes an immediate impression over the synched intro animation and menu loop. The 2003 *Led Zeppelin* DVD uses songs and previously unseen footage as accompaniment to its motion menus. The Special Collector's Edition DVD of Sergio Leone's classic Western *Once Upon a Time in the West* runs the trademark sound of a squeaking windmill over the menu options, taken straight from the opening sequence. This referencing of sound is a direct parallel to the process used in assembling the graphic elements of a menu. Both set the tone and give the viewer an impression of what is to come in the main feature.

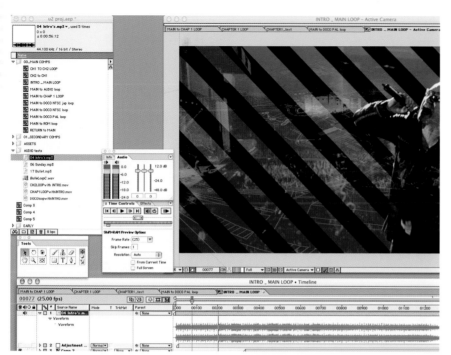

Left: *After Effects was used to create an animated sequence leading into the main menu for the U2 Go Home DVD. The sequence was synchronized with a section of audio, the U2 song 'Bullet the Blue Sky', which determined the pacing. Key moments were introduced according to the music, such as each part of the title coming in on drumbeats.*

Both sound and vision set the tone and give the viewer an impression of what is to come

Right: *The main menu for this collection of live material by New Order used the group's anthemic song 'Blue Monday' as the background audio. The vertical colour lines in the menu were made to move in time to the music using a Motion Math tool in After Effects. This allows the audio values to be applied to Motion, Opacity, and Scale properties.*

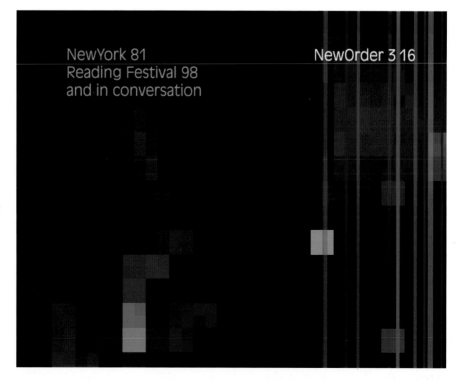

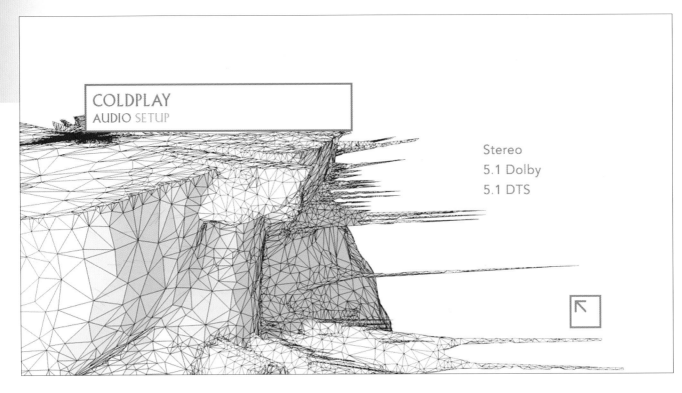

COLDPLAY
AUDIO SETUP

Stereo
5.1 Dolby
5.1 DTS

Formats and authoring

All audio files in a project have to be in the same initial format, such as AIFF and so on. Desktop authoring packages such as Apple's A.Pack can convert the sound in your main DVD footage to compatible formats such as PCM, MPEG-2, or Dolby Digital AC-3. Furthermore, some applications, such as DVD Studio Pro, allow audio files that are attached to video assets to be automatically assigned to the same motion menu. Of course, you can also assign audio files to both still and motion menus the manual way.

Some designers build up the audio for menus in After Effects or a similar application. With transition and intro sequences, this has the benefit of showing where the audio will interact with the menu animation. Compositing applications allow you to manipulate layered sound files in the same way as image layers – you can apply filters and effects to create interesting audio for spot sound effects. The length of the audio file can determine the length of the animation, with the two being adjusted together in the same After Effects composition. Once the composition is complete, the audio file can be rendered out separately.

Rules for adding audio

Like everything else when it comes to authoring DVD menus, there are a few guidelines to follow when adding audio.

Although you can add up to eight tracks of audio, the DVD player can only play one at a time: the audio tracks do

Above: *The audio attached to the menus in the* Coldplay Live 2003 *DVD by Abbey Road Interactive was drawn from a selection of tunes lifted from the concert on the disc. These were treated with reverb effects to create an unusual echo sound, almost as if the viewer were outside the venue. This concept was well suited to the menu system as in a sense the viewer is outside the concert while using the menus. It also hints at the full audio experience to be savoured when the user chooses to watch the content. Keeping usability and design rules in mind, the audio was made subtle enough so as not to irritate the viewer during repetitive menu loops.*

not supplement the main audio, but are played instead of it. When designing a language option menu screen, you should include a button for each dubbed language and also a button to return the viewer to the main menu. On this kind of menu, make a note of the track number of each language as, in order to keep things consistent throughout the DVD, you need to place audio files of the same language on the same number audio track throughout all timelines.

You should also make sure the background music matches the theme and tone of the DVD. Heavy rock guitar tracks will not sit well on a wedding video, for example, unless of course the participants have taken that as the theme for the wedding as a whole.

DVD audio has safe areas, too, though in terms of time rather than space. Some DVD players clip the audio at the beginning of a menu or transition,

so it's advisable to begin the audio at about 10 frames into the animation to ensure it runs smoothly.

Although you can add audio to both still and motion menus, assigning music to a still menu screen can cause problems when you want to move onto the next submenu. Viewers will encounter a break in the sound as the player moves to the next menu where a new audio track begins. Whatever the type of menu, make sure your audio is of a sufficient length so as not to start repeating right away. This can become tiresome very quickly. Tracks should be at least a minute in length and should definitely not be shorter than any motion or animation loop in your menus.

It's better to use more atmospheric or ambient pieces of music for background audio as this reduces the irritability factor. An instrumental extract is always more advisable than a vocal or

'busy' piece of music it also has the advantage that you can edit the loop point in more easily. Audio on menus can also become irritating if constantly on a loop, so on some discs, the audio is set to play once and then is not repeated on further loops.

Unlike CD-authoring, audio on DVD has to be saved at 48kHz, which you'll need to remember when you are preparing your audio and video footage. Another factor to consider is the volume of your menu. The audio level shouldn't be louder than the level set for the main feature. Returning to a loud menu after watching the programme is intensely irritating. Remember, also, to keep the level consistent throughout your menu system.

Left: *Some designers will build up audio in a specialized application, such as Adobe Audition. Part of Adobe's Video Collection, it contains features that assist with the development of sound for video.*

Adding subtitles

Subtitles are not just for the hard of hearing. They can add a new commercial element to your DVD. As well as dialogue translation, they can be used to add commentary or notes regarding the content on screen. Of course, you also have the option to add closed captions for deaf or disabled users. Rather than confine yourself to a transcript of the words spoken on screen, you can include sound effects and additional information to make the whole experience more accessible and enjoyable.

Most DVD authoring software applications offer some sort of subtitling feature. A few are simple text editing tools, but the majority of professional applications have advanced subtitling support for this important part of the authoring process.

In most applications, subtitles are not treated as menu elements – they are more akin to a video or graphics track, overlaying the video footage. For this reason, they can be more versatile than menus: the designer can add logo graphics and simple animation. As such, they can provide a variety of information to aid your presentation, including statistics and trivia.

Left: *A stylized treatment of the subtitle screen of O Brother, Where Art Thou?, created by ARI. The design is based around a radio reminiscent of the period in which the movie is set. A flick-switch option sets the English subtitles on or off.*

Subtitling a whole movie is a long and arduous process, which is best left to a professional subtitling agency if you can afford it. But for a corporate presentation, to accompany interview footage or a documentary, it is possible to produce a text file of reasonable length in a word processing application. This can then be imported into the application. Obviously, accurate timing is vital. Professional applications like Adobe Encore DVD and Apple's Studio Pro can handle up to 32 subtitle tracks (16 tracks for widescreen video), though the DVD player will only read one at a time. It is practical, therefore, for a menu to be used to give the user the option of selecting a subtitle track, whether it's a commentary track or dialogue translation. If only one language is offered, menu buttons are still required to switch the subtitles on and off.

Accurate timing is vital

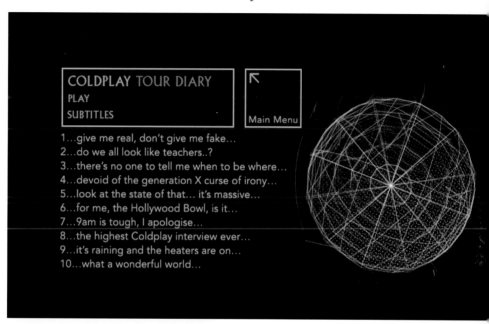

In conversation

subtitles English German All subtitles off ↗

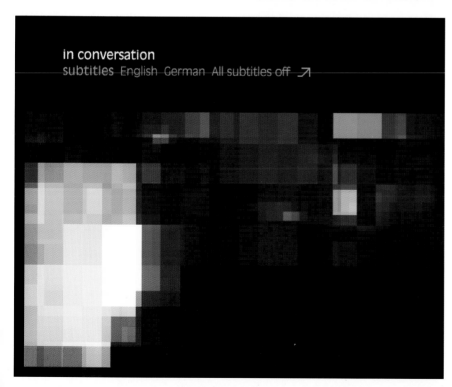

Left: *For the New Order 3 16 DVD, subtitles were available in English and German to run alongside an interview with the band. The menu screen consisted of bright colours against black to capture the essence of the main concert. As the background had a random feel and the colours were sharp and bright, it would have been difficult to ensure that the options were always visible, so areas of pure black were used to lay out the text.*

Above: *For the Coldplay Live 2003 DVD, the subtitles option appears alongside the Tour Diary. The subtitles' submenu directly relates to the documentary and not to the concert, so was designed against black to reflect the fact that the content was different from the main feature. The wireframe, 3D, spinning globe was created in Infini-D and helped to get across the 'world tour' theme visually, with rapidly moving particle lines suggesting the various routes taken on the tour.*

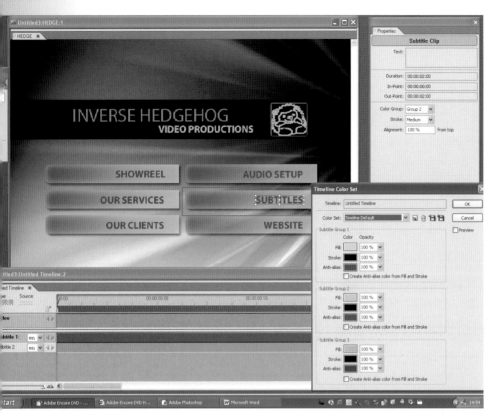

Above: *In Encore DVD, you set up subtitle selection via a button property that you set along with the button's destination link. Although you specify the tracks with the destination link, the track choices are a DVD-wide setting. After the viewer activates the button, the track setting remains in effect for all subsequently viewed timelines, unless the viewer resets it manually.*

You can import subtitle text and time codes from a plain text file or use the application's subtitle editor to format and synchronize it to the video track. You can also enter them directly on top of the video or image, and set them to begin at a moment defined by the position of the playhead on the timeline. For example, Adobe Encore DVD lets you create subtitles either by typing them into the Monitor window or importing them from an external file. Subtitle import formats can include text script files, Image Script, and FAB Images format files. Image-based subtitles created outside Encore are imported into the application as a full-size graphic with an alpha channel.Unless they are a text script file, you cannot edit them within the application, but you need to format and position subtitles in a text script as a group when you import them as they contain no screen position or formatting information.

All subtitle tracks are in the form of a separate overlay and are not part of the DVD's video stream. As such, they can be switched on and off, with several different subtitles tracks appearing at different times over the same piece of video. Authoring applications like Encore also feature each screen of subtitles as a separate clip in the Timeline. This separation means that you can use the subtitle tracks to add in pointers or build up animated elements on top of video, adding short subtitle clips incrementally to give a semblance of movement. However, using a graphics-heavy animation in the subtitle track can significantly affect the playback of the video, due to the impact on the bit rate of the video stream.

Depending on your system and its support for multiple language characters, you can enter text in any language you want into the various subtitle tracks. Some applications allow you to apply extensive formatting and effects to the subtitles within the limitations of the DVD specification. You can even copy and paste subtitle clips, complete with formatting, into other streams or tracks in the timeline.

Rules to remember
Like many other aspects of the DVD menu process, working with subtitles has its limitations. For example, as subtitles are overlaid on the video, they can lose synchronicity with the accompanying audio. You don't want the

wrong subtitles to appear under your footage, so correct timing is a necessity. To synchronize elements of video, graphics, and audio in video and DVD authoring, we can make use of timecode. This is the standard method of associating each frame of video with a unique time-based identifier (according to hours:minutes:seconds:frames). Material brought in from a video editing application will already have timecode associated with it, and this will be displayed in the timeline of the DVD application. Text files contain timecode for the start and end of each subtitle.

As they are just like subpicture overlays, subtitle tracks carry the same restrictions. They are limited to a palette of three colours – mapping to the fill, the outline, and the partial anti-aliasing of the characters. Encore DVD allows a choice of one of three user-defined groups of colours for each timeline at any one time and these are defined using the *Timeline Color Set* dialog box. With other applications, such as Studio Pro, the three text colours are assigned to the text colour, the first outline and a second outline used as text border to improve the contrast with the video.

So although different methods seem to be used by various packages, the result and conventions are basically the same. A fourth colour is also usually used as the background and is normally transparent, with its *Opacity* set to 0. You can use different colour groups to vary the subtitles and to help identify or distinguish between subtitles (to identify different speakers, for example).

Left: *Studio Pro has an* Inspector *palette to select and adjust the three-colour combination used for subtitle text. A fourth colour is kept transparent to be used as the background.*

Showcase
My Little Eye (Special Edition)

When the designers at DVD authoring facility The Pavement were given the brief to design 'the most interactive DVD in the world', they pulled out all the stops to create something special for *My Little Eye*.

Is this the most interactive DVD menu in the world?

DVD interaction is, for the most part, a series of pages and video clips linked together by buttons. As we've seen, the viewer's experience can be enhanced with transitions, subpictures, and conditional branching. For the DVD release of *My Little Eye*, however, something much more groundbreaking was called for. The film's premise lent itself spectactulary well to a more interactive film encounter.

The Pavement's Lloyd Shaer explains the approach taken by his team when faced with such a challenging design brief: 'We didn't know if interactivity would help sell more discs or not but it was great from the point of view that we could really go for it.'

Always eager to 'cross the red line' of the DVD format, the staff at The Pavement are well aware of the constraints of DVD as a medium. The actual elements of the disc in themselves were never going to make the disc unique or groundbreaking.

Lloyd explains how The Pavement used DVD design and authoring skills to make the DVD special: 'To put it in perspective, most menus are 30 to 90 seconds long. In the case of the *League*

of Gentlemen, the menu was 3 minutes. You're never going to get an intro that lasts longer than that. What was groundbreaking about *My Little Eye* was that we actually did a full-length feature menu. That's what's important.'

Below: *The feature movie plays in a window within the specially designed Web-style interface. The menu's graphics update as the narrative unfolds.*

Design principles

Faking an online browser in a DVD menu
The menu of *My Little Eye* was designed as an interactive Web browser, to tie in with the movie's webcam-related subject matter. Once the user has opted to watch the film in this interactive browser mode, the usual rules of DVD watching, like jumping to other chapters, no longer apply. Lloyd: 'Once the DVD viewer is in the enhanced interactive menu, they can't get to certain features when they want. They have to wait. The whole point of *My Little Eye* was that it was a kind of *Big Brother* thing. You have to watch as though a website voyeur and wait for the narrative to go through the motions. That was the basic principle of the disc. Although it is a movie, we tried to give the user the feeling that they were actually watching events online.'

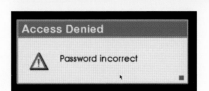

Left: *To enhance the interactive version of My Little Eye, the DVD user has to mimic the scene in the movie where a character enters a credit card number to access a sinister snuff website. The user is faced with an interface containing a blank credit card field. Using the handheld remote, the*

Right: *If the numbers entered aren't correct, the user is taken to an alternative graphic that looks identical to the original submit page. However, pressing submit on this page will link them to another page containing a graphic displaying the words 'Access Denied'. Clicking on this graphic returns the user to the first page of the credit card menu. When all four numbers are entered correctly, the user is granted full access to the enhanced interactive menu.*

user of the DVD has to 'type' in a code that is hidden on the reverse of the DVD sleeve. As each correct letter is typed in, an asterix appears in the field.

A version of this interactive log-on effect can be recreated in any high-end authoring package. First, create different versions of the interface. Version one should have a blank field. Version 2 should be identical aside from displaying an asterix to indicate that a number has been entered. You can then build buttons over the relevant entry numbers to make the DVD jump to the next graphic in the sequence.

Left: *Once the interactive browser is activated, the main feature plays within a smaller window in the browser-style interface. The characters from the movie appear in their respective contestant icons. The effect of each character materializing within their blank icon mimics the effect of a jpeg downloading over a slow Web connection. This effect can be achieved by using your DVD authoring software to play a short movie clip within each icon.*

Viewer choice

Although a feature-length interactive menu helps make the viewer of the *My Little Eye* DVD feel like part of the movie (albeit as a voyeur watching from multiple web-cams!), the Pavement's designers had to take into account the fact that not everyone would want to interact with the movie in this way. This is something you have to bear in mind when designing your own discs.

Lloyd: 'In the case of *My Little Eye*'s menu, you have two choices. Instead of the interactive option, you can just go in and watch the movie. If someone just wants to go into the disc, watch the feature, and get some extras, then you've got to give that option to them. They've got to get to the content easily, simply, and quickly, otherwise they'll get very frustrated. The novelty of a complex menu actually wears off quite quickly.'

Instant access

As *My Little Eye*'s narrative unfolds, the unlucky web-cast contestants finally locate the website that is showing their every move to unseen voyeurs. They discover a webpage that assigns icons to each contestant. Rather alarmingly, each picture displays the odds of that particular character surviving. The odds are being constantly updated, allowing the users of the website to make bets on who dies next. The designers at The Pavement incorporated this website design into their interactive DVD menu. The DVD user can interrupt the movie to access extra information about any of the housemates by clicking on the relevant character's icon. This triggers the DVD to play bonus material like the audition tapes made by the character to get into the house. When a contestant dies during the movie, their icon in the DVD menu changes colour, mimicking

the behaviour of the icons on the sinister snuff website. The interactive DVD menu also uses the Camera Angle option to allow the user to jump between seeing the movie within the browser-style interface to display the movie in full screen mode. To enhance the difference between Web and full-screen mode, the sound changes from a 2 channel stereo mix to the full 5.1 mix.

Technical versus creative

Creating a design that complements the style of the movie is not a new thing. However, making the menu give the DVD user a sense that they are part of the narrative (even if it's a sinister voyeur betting on the demise of a bunch of teenagers) adds an extra dimension to the DVD experience. At certain points while watching the interactive menu, you can jump to alternative camera angles, and even hear what viewers of

Left: *This kind of fully interactive menu is not for everyone. You have to give the user the option to watch the movie and access the deleted scenes in the traditional way.*

'The novelty of a complex menu actually wears off quite quickly.'

Right; *The interactive browser mode adds extra layers to the film. Pressing the remote's audio button at certain times allows you to hear the company operatives using their walkie-talkies, a feature not available to viewers of the theater version of the movie.*

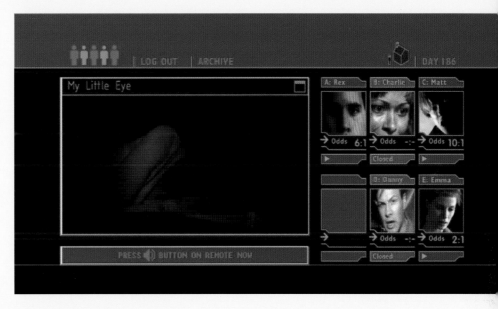

'The designers at The Pavement added extra layers of narrative information'

the theater version couldn't hear – the company operatives talking to each other via walkie-talkie. By making the DVD interactive on so many levels, the designers of The Pavement have added extra layers of narrative information for the benefit of those watching the DVD version. This type of interaction encourages sales as the DVD viewers are getting a unique experience that wasn't available to those who saw the movie at the cinema.

The DVD medium places undeniable constraints on creating such an interactive disc. Luckily, the fact the interactive browser was meant to be streaming from a website meant that The Pavement could use a lower bit rate to fit the additional video material onto the disc. Technical constraints such as disc space should always be taken into account when designing a menu, but in this case it's absolutely critical.

Lloyd again: 'This is what's important about the programmers working with the creatives. You wouldn't have got the *My Little Eye* special edition if you'd just gone to a creative or just gone to a programmer. Normally, I'll chuck out an idea to Sebastian, our head technical guy. If I see the eyebrows go up I'll know it's a possibility. If I see a frown I know it's not going to happen.'

DVD as part of the movie

Whether *My Little Eye* met the brief to be 'the most interactive disc in the world' or not, there's no doubt that it pushes the technical and creative boundaries of the medium. 'The label were happy with the interactive browser', says Lloyd. 'More importantly, the director and the producer were over the moon. They felt that it finished the movie off. In the beginning, DVD was like VHS; it enabled you to watch a film. Now it's

starting to become important to think about the DVD when you start to think about the movie shoot. People are actually starting to invest serious money into the making of a DVD because they realize that it's an important part of the film industry. That's why we get to work on some really nice projects.'

5

innovation

Great ideas to make your DVD different

What makes a great DVD? Obviously the quality of the picture and the sound are major factors, but viewers also get excited by great menu design and especially any extras. It's a good idea to add some special features to your menu to make it just that little bit different.

Adding extra interactive features, animated elements, specially designed sound effects, or hidden menus and content will not suit every production. You don't need to add hidden elements to a corporate presentation DVD, for example, and if you did, you would probably make the user want to switch off. However, it is more or less de rigueur for movie DVD releases these days to include some extras on a menu, and even the most basic DVD menu – where the huge quantities of 'behind the scenes' features that many commercial DVDs take for granted aren't available – can be lifted to new heights by adding a few trimmings.

Right: *For* Amelie, *created for Momentum in the UK, designer Luke Tilly included a hidden feature to chart the travels of a garden gnome in the film. The Station menu, adapted from film footage, had a hidden button next to the gnome in the shop window. If this was discovered by the user, they would uncover a menu featuring a world map with selectable locations. Each location featured a polaroid of the tourist gnome posing in front of a world landmark.*

Games

DVD games are subject to authoring restrictions that confine the user to take a predetermined path. This means that they are very basic compared to a fully interactive console game, where the player has a specialized controller and complete interaction with the gameplay. Even so, a game that is designed well can be a good interactive element to add to a DVD menu, and many are found on DVDs aimed at the children's market.

Most DVD games have to be based around a multiple-choice system, which restricts the amount of possible outcomes or variables. If this were not the case, menu authors would need to create transitions or screens for an almost limitless amount of possibilities.

Fortunately, multiple choice is a natural fit for quiz games, which make for some simple fun when the film is over.

audio
direction?   1 . . . . 2 . . . . 3 . . . . 4 . . . . 5 6

go

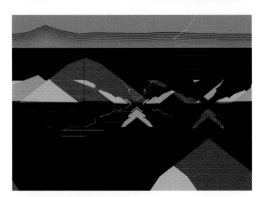

Deconstructing
the innovative menu

Commercial DVD designers come up
with creative menu ideas all the time.
Viewers enjoy alternative main menus,
immersive environments for menu
navigation, interesting audio effects, and
hidden features. Deconstructing some
innovative professional designs may
provide you with the inspiration to add
that little something to your project.
Let's take an in-depth look at one DVD
that manages to cram in most of the
creative ideas listed above. This is the
menu system that ARI devised for *So
Solid Crew*. Determined to make full use
of the medium's interactive capabilities,
ARI proposed that this menu feature the
band playing a gig in an underground
parking ramp, which suits the urban
nature of their music.

Left: *As part of a
cover-mounted DVD
for* Creative Review
*magazine, Andy Potts
created games based
on the themes of the
issue. As one of the
themes was 'sound',
Potts designed a maze
game called MZ, which
is based on the idea of
collecting layers of
audio in order to
escape the labyrinth.
The game player
watches an animation
that constitutes a
sequence of six remote
control directions,
which the viewer needs
to memorize in order
to get through the
maze. The user has to
select the first
direction from a
possible four on the
remote control — if
they select the correct
one, it triggers a
progressive animation
through the maze, on
to the next choice of
four. If they select the
wrong direction, a
Game Over animation
is triggered. At the end
of the maze game, the
user is treated to an
animation of the band
escaping the maze,
playing as one tune
the six pieces of audio
they gather en route.*

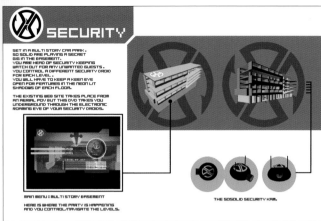

SECURITY

SET IN A MULTI STORY CAR PARK.
SO SOLID ARE PLAYING A SECRET
GIG IN THE BASEMENT.
YOU ARE HEAD OF SECURITY KEEPING
WATCH OUT FOR ANY UNWANTED GUESTS.
YOU CONTROL A DIFFERENT SECURITY DROID
FOR EACH LEVEL.
YOU WILL HAVE TO KEEP A KEEN EYE
OPEN FOR FEATURES IN THE NEON LIT
SHADOWS OF EACH FLOOR.

THE EXISTING WEB SITE TAKES PLACE FROM
AN AERIAL POV BUT THIS DVD TAKES YOU
UNDERGROUND THROUGH THE ELECTRONIC
ROAMING EYE OF YOUR SECURITY DROIDS.

MAIN MENU : MULTI STORY BASEMENT

HERE IS WHERE THE PARTY IS HAPPENING
AND YOU CONTROL/NAVIGATE THE LEVELS.

THE SOSOLID SECURITY KAM.

Left: *The initial concept was that the viewer would take the place of So Solid's head of security and follow the action through the eyes of security camera droids. The design team wanted to split the content across different floors of the parking ramp and have the cameras navigate around the menu system, presenting the options as digital readouts laid over the camera viewpoint. This approach certainly differed from the normal use of interactivity in DVD menus and called for certain menu constructs to be designed, including smooth flowing transitions and moving menus.*

Right: *The main content of the DVD is a filmed concert, a documentary, and a selection of promotional videos. Linking transitions take the form of the camera droids, who roam between the content. For the chapter screens along the length of each floor, two other camera droids were included so that the user can switch to either of these, reducing the amount of complicated transitions needed. The parking ramp was constructed using 3ds max, and 3D cars were created to fill various spaces, with footage thumbnails projected on their windshields. Camera move animations and pivoting camera droids were added before everything was composited with the background in After Effects.*

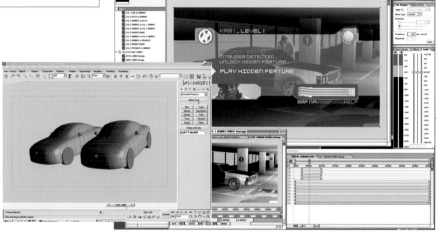

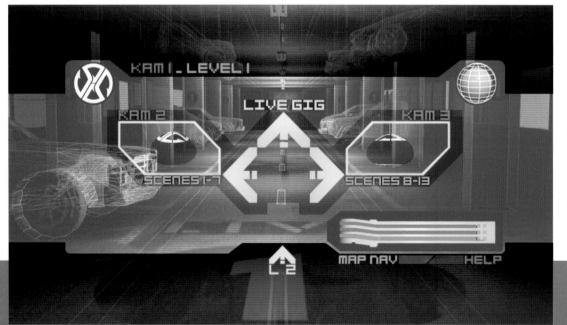

Left: *The navigation device was based around a standard DVD remote control layout. The main menu lets you access everything on that level – for instance, the Live Gig or chapters on Level 1 – or enables you to move up to Level 2.*

Right: *Each level has hidden features that can be discovered by the user, and elaborate animations were added to access them. These consist of extra tracks or outtakes from the documentary and, in keeping with the security theme, were designed around the idea of an intruder alert. Other menus were designed to contain only hidden features and the user* *has to search the area for content among some crates or two empty cars.*

Left: *An innovative feature of the menu is its dual navigation system. After developing the complex interfaces and transitions, the designers realized that the user might want to 'cut to the chase' and bypass the animations to get to the content. A more traditional* *interface was therefore designed, called Map Nav. This interface is accessible from every menu, and lays out the options from each level as clearly as possible. It also allows the user to return to the 'parking ramp' at any time. A help page was also made available.*

Right: *ARI also developed special audio effects for the menu system. When the user is on Level 1 of the virtual environment, clear audio tracks loop to denote proximity to the main concert footage. However, as the user moves through the environment, the audio gets more muffled with distance, adding to the atmosphere generated by the visuals. Spot effects were also added for animations on visual displays and for the movement of* *the animated camera droids. Voices of the band members had to be overlaid and be clearly audible as they were instructive in content. All the audio was brought together in AE and synched up visually to the menus.*

DVD-ROM

If you are serious about creating a DVD menu with a difference, you may want to consider adding extra material to the disc that doesn't fall into the multimedia category. For this you need to create a separate section of your DVD that a computer can read – this is known as DVD-ROM or Hybrid DVD. DVD-Video discs contain VIDEO-TS and AUDIO-TS folders only, while a DVD-ROM will also contain folders of other files. These could be back-up materials for your content, video files, or scripts, and information in text or PDF formats.

Consumer DVD players will ignore DVD-ROM material, but this has advantages. For one, since the DVD-ROM section will be played on a PC, you can include Flash or Shockwave animations and games. Remember that more data files in the ROM section means less space for video and audio, so use formats that take up the least space – JPEG for images, Flash or SVG for vector animation, TXT files for text, and so on.

Place your DVD-ROM files in a separate directory or volume and be sure to give the DVD volume a name, using the *Properties* or *Inspectors* within your DVD application. If you don't, the computer will just display the disc as DVD-Volume on the desktop and you'll never be able to change it. You can also add notes and author information for the disc's *Properties* dialog at this point.

If you have extra material on your disc, include a submenu in the DVD-Video portion that lists the DVD-ROM content; most users won't put the disc into a PC without a good reason. Create a special button on the main menu to alert users to the fact that this ROM content exists – there's no point in going to all this effort if nobody gets to see it.

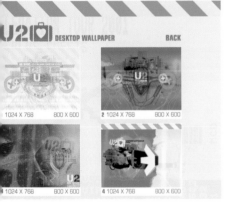

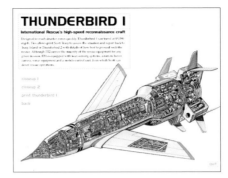

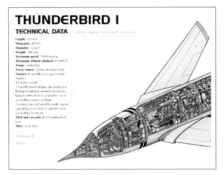

Left and below: *For the Thunderbirds DVD series (eight discs in all), the ROM section includes a detailed technical drawing of one of the Thunderbird vessels, featuring a different ship for each disc. The PC is able to display these highly detailed drawings in a way that a DVD menu cannot. The amount of detail in the images would be lost on a television screen, and having the content on the ROM section allows the user to click areas of the vehicle to bring up descriptions as rollover tags, just like live elements on a website. This kind of functionality just isn't available on DVD-Video and this amount of text on a TV screen would be impractical.*

Links to the Thunderbirds and Carlton (the production company) websites are also included on the DVD.

Opposite and above: *The DVD-ROM section on the U2 Go Home title features a lot of exclusive content and is a real bonus for U2 fans. The band's Slane concert was filmed with special 360-degree cameras and the ROM section includes this footage. It's in the form of a QuickTime VR movie, which allows the user to rotate the view of the camera with their mouse. Other files include an exclusive Tour Diary calendar and clock that can be left on your computer desktop. If the date on the computer corresponds with a particular tour date, information about the gig and venue is displayed. There's also a selection of animated screensavers and wallpapers, all designed to be consistent with the DVD menus.*

Get yourself connected

Another innovative feature that you can include on a DVD-ROM is the provision of Web links or hyperlinks. This allows you to set markers in your DVD content that, when reached, will launch a website if the user is online, prepare an email message, or open a document stored on the DVD itself. This has all sorts of implications, not least a massive leap in interactivity and the ability to program in access to supplementary material for your DVD users. The Web offers its own kind of interactivity and is more suited to text-heavy content and quick access to images. Movie and record companies often build mini websites or microsites based on the DVD release, which can only be accessed from a link on the DVD. This type of multi-platform content viewing is becoming more popular, and the user benefits from the various interactive strengths of each medium.

A cross-platform version of this Web link feature exists, called DVD@CCESS, which can be authored using DVD Studio Pro. Links are activated automatically when the Hybrid DVD is played on Apple's DVD player, but Windows computers are required to install an application to process the links – this is bundled automatically in the ROM section during authoring. This feature is also enabled in Roxio Toast Titanium, which is mainly intended for the creation of CD and DVD-ROM discs, but also has the capacity to create DVD-VIDEO discs with simple menus.

DVD@CCESS hasn't been a huge success on the PC, as some DVD@CCESS links have been reported to perform badly on some Windows-based machines, or just not work at all.

One alternative is PCFriendly, which has now been superseded by InterActual Player. Incorporated into many PC-based DVD authoring tools including those by Sonic Solutions and Daikin, this technology is used on many Hollywood movie titles to allow users to connect to the Web from the DVD menu.

Whatever kind it is, all technology that introduces Web links to DVD obviously relies on the correct naming of files and folders. It is very important to give the DVD itself a name in order to provide a base reference for the file structure.

COLDPLAY EXTRAS
WEBLINKS

Insert this DVD into your PC to access weblinks to the following sites.

Make Trade Fair	www.maketradefair.com
Environmental News Network	www.enn.com
Amnesty International	www.amnesty.org
Oxfam	www.oxfam.org
Greenpeace	www.greenpeace.org
WaterAid	www.wateraid.org.uk
Planet Save	www.planetsave.com
Crisis	www.crisis.org.uk
Carbon Neutral	www.futureforests.com

Above: *ARI's menus for the* Coldplay Live 2003 *DVD employs innovative methods in its use of the various platforms and technologies. In doing so, it gets across as much content as possible and offers the user many levels of interactivity.*

Menu button
The Web links page on the main Coldplay DVD menu contains information on how to access the PC elements on the disc and a list of the Web addresses, but not the live links, as these are available on the DVD-ROM section.

The Web offers its own kind of interactivity and is more suited to text-heavy content and quick access to images

Left: Coldplay Live 2003 has a small ROM element that contains live Web links. The DVD ROM contains a launcher screen that opens the Web links page or allows you to access the DVD player directly.

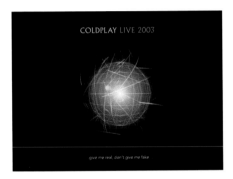

Left: *A great deal of rich media content is included on a Web microsite that is only accessible by those who purchase the DVD. This microsite has additional footage from television appearances and smaller gigs that were deemed too poor in resolution quality to go on the DVD, but suit a downloadable format such as Windows Media. There are also photographs, text, and additional artwork that is of great interest to fans, as well as downloadable wallpapers and screensavers, specially designed to accompany the DVD release.*

Above: *An accompanying audio CD features a CD-ROM portion with numerous gallery photographs that aren't included in the main DVD portion.*

Multi-angle and mixed angle DVD

DVD has some great advantages over tape-based or linear media. One is, of course, its storage capacity. Another is the option it gives the user to access any part of the disc at any time. A unique feature that derives from this non-linear access is the ability to switch between multiple tracks of content, such as the use of multiple angles during live concert footage.

Right: *For the live DVD for the band Five, ARI included a menu to allow the viewer to choose a multi-angle version of two songs. A camera was trained on each performer during the two tracks and five menu buttons were created for each. Video footage was grabbed from the multiple tracks and played on a loop to provide motion menu buttons.*

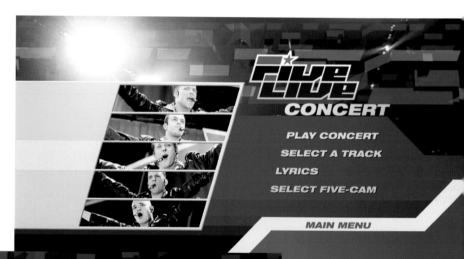

COLDPLAY LIVE 2003
MULTI-ANGLE

Daylight
God Put A Smile Upon
Your Face
Trouble

In My Place

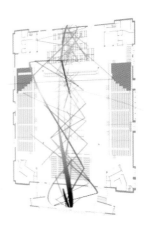

The option to change perspective can enliven any DVD, allowing viewers to follow their favourite musician during songs at a concert, or keep a favourite player in frame during a sports DVD. Movie DVDs may also include sequences where you the viewer can choose between shots themselves, or view 'before' and 'after' versions of special effects. As well as multi-angle, you can have mixed angle tracks on your disc, where the video track runs as normal but switches to alternative tracks and angles at prearranged times. This takes up less space than the multi-angle approach as the extra tracks you have to include need only be the length of the alternate sections, whereas for multi-angles, you have to provide individual full-length alternative tracks to allow the user to switch angles when they want.

To author such content you obviously need to make use of more than one camera when filming the event, unless you want to offer something like alternative music videos to the same audio track. Whatever the format, the next stage is to edit the footage into synchronized tracks (including audio).

Here you make use of Timecode-based tools in a non-linear editing application such as Premiere, Final Cut Pro, or Pinnacle Studio, then export them individually as DVD-friendly MPEG-2 files. There are some restrictions when you take these files into an authoring application, such as DVD Studio Pro. All tracks for use in multi-angle streams must be exactly the same length, resolution, frame rate, and encoding bit rate. The Group of Pictures (GOP) sequence defined as a result of the MPEG encoding process must have the same structure and should be in the same MPEG format. Mixed angle streams require the same length of track for the alternative sections. Each DVD authoring application will have a different method of interleaving these tracks into the multiple streams of the DVD timeline, but we will concentrate here on accessing them from within the menu system. Be aware, however, that multiple angle support is not found on all authoring applications and tends to be confined to the more professional packages such as Studio Pro and Sonic Scenarist.

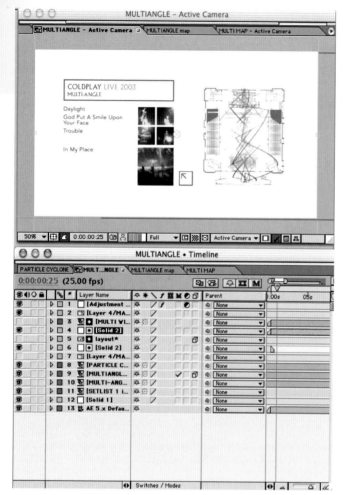

Above: *To create an appropriate background for the* Coldplay Live 2003 *multi-angle menu, the designer requested a blueprint-style drawing of the concert venue. From this, he conveyed the concept by creating a 3D model of angled lines on a rotation loop and combining it with the blueprints in After Effects.*

SPRM

The DVD specification allows for up to nine multi-angle MPEG video streams, including the main menu stream, which you switch between in sequence using the angle button on the remote control. The DVD player operates according to a strict set of system parameters that keep a register of the status of the player – these are known as SPRMs and, among other things, control what language is in use, which subtitle track is active and, in a similar fashion, which angle is being viewed. The SPRM 3 value holds the designation of the current stream being played – in a range from 1 to 9, where 1 is the default track if there is only one angle. By using your DVD authoring package and the DVD player's ability to access this information, you can set up your menu to display button highlights or provide other feedback when the viewer switches angles on the remote control.

Planning for multi-angles

Although you should always plan your DVD menu before you start, when you enter the world of multiple angles and mixed tracks, it is even more important to have a design worked out or chaos will ensue. For one thing, you're certainly going to have more than one or two buttons on your multi-angle menu screens. With up to nine angles to choose from for each track, you are in danger of swamping your viewer with options. Simplicity is best, so keep this in mind when designing your layouts.

When laying out the main menu, provide a separate button link to the multiple-angle menu page. You then need to provide buttons linked to each of the separate tracks. Remember to provide a button to return to the angle selection page. More tracks also mean more space, which should be remembered when you are budgeting for disc space and working out bit rate constraints. Another thing to remember is that only one audio stream can accompany each video angle.

For mixed angle tracks, you need to assign chapter markers in the timeline to the places where you want the alternative material to begin. Link the menu button to the first video stream or to the start of the track to make sure this is the first play part of the sequence. All the alternative streams should be aligned to the marker where the angle tracks are positioned, ready to be played according to the angle set by the user. Options like the *Story* function in Studio Pro can be used to arrange the playback

of the track according to the position of the chapter markers, while further customization using multiple angles is possible by using the scripting abilities of professional authoring applications. You can assign a menu button for each alternate story – this will begin with the first play sequence then seamlessly drop in the corresponding alternative stream at the correct point. As such, it is ideal when you are dealing with different viewpoints of a wedding or business presentation, or even to provide alternative endings to your home movies.

Below: *The DVD of concert footage created by ARI for* Eurythmics: Peace *shares the same menu design principles as the* Five Live *DVD, this time providing alternate footage of the two main band members for two songs.*

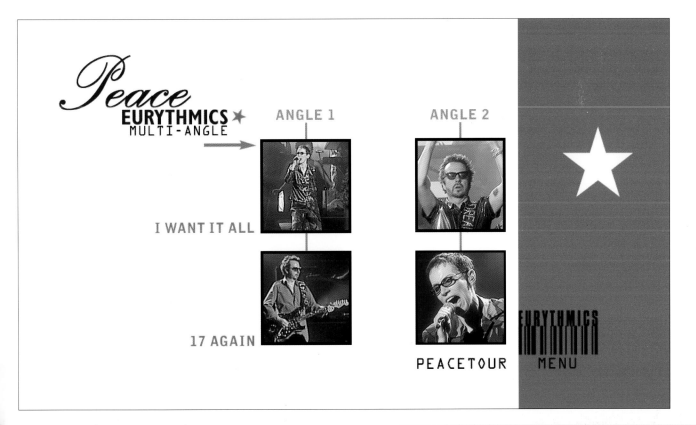

How design and interaction work together

Any interactive medium relies on good design for the user to get the most out of it, and nowhere is this more evident than in interface design. Interfaces such as DVD menus need to guide the viewer to the content, so designers create prominent buttons at the highest level of the menu to take the user to the most important and relevant areas of the disc. As we have discussed already, the colour and alignment of menu elements also highlights the importance of content, and the direction the viewer should be taking.

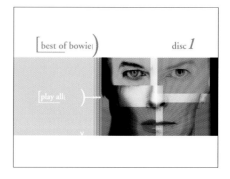

Designing for interactivity, or interaction design as it is generally known, is an artistic discipline all of its own. According to its leading exponents, an interface should contain at least four qualities – the viewer should be able to interact with it, its functions should be easy to understand, these functions should work as expected, and the user should receive feedback.

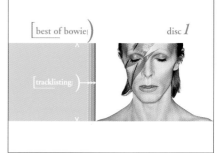

Let's look at some DVD menus that show design and interaction working together. The DVD menus for *This is Stina Nordenstam* and the two-disc *Best of Bowie* set, both designed by ARI, have no subpictures and only one option per menu. Instead, they use a type of image swapping where the main image changes in response to user interaction.

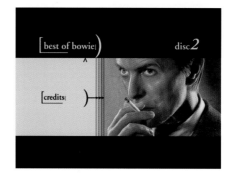

Above and left:
With the menu for the David Bowie DVD, the user can select up or down on the remote to trigger a transition animation. This alters the image of David Bowie on the right, while the text animates to form a new option. The design is laid out in such a way that it shows a direct response to user interaction, which proved to be a highly successful approach for this DVD.

Left: *The use of Victorian-style circus posters featuring ornate styling and performing animals establishes a look and feel for this music DVD. The unusual navigation comprises individual selectable items, each with its own still menu design. For the majority of the menu screens, there are no subpictures at all. Instead, the user presses left or right on the remote control, causing the still menu to change to another static image. The designs for each video selection are essentially the same, but each has a different background colour and is linked to a particular circus element, with the name of the video under a screenshot in the centre. As well as creating an effect reminiscent of a Victorian picture diorama to prompt the user through the menu, this is a very effective way to bypass the restrictive, sometimes ugly, subpicture overlay method, and to inject variety into the design.*

Right: *As the key demographic target for the So Solid Crew DVD is the PlayStation 2 generation, ARI decided that the interface should follow the intricate stylings of hi-tech computer games, featuring lots of moving elements and information as well as having a 'robot camera' viewpoint. In a move to facilitate interaction, the floors were colour coded green, red, and blue to help the user navigate. Footage of two members of So Solid Crew was also added to the menus, giving instructions on the content of a particular floor or general location reminders. The cameras that move around the environment are accompanied by audio feedback, which gives the user an idea of which way to go for different content – if the viewer wants to experience the live gig, they know to head for the areas where the background music is louder.*

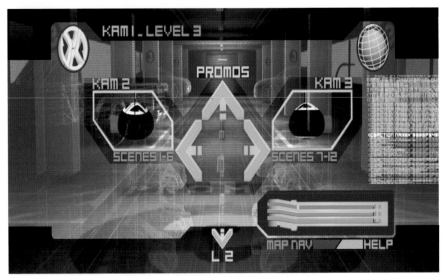

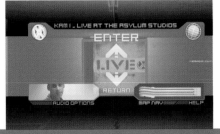

Right: *For the special features menu of O Brother, Where Art Thou?, ARI decided to recreate a scene from the movie. In this scene, the character is seeking a certain hair product, called Dapper Dan. To the character's disappointment, the storekeeper uses extendable grippers to bring a can of hair pomade called Fop down from a high shelf. Andy Potts created a shelf full of pomade tins to represent the separate features while the Dapper Dan tin was reserved as a gateway to return to the main menu.*

To create this menu, the designer took a grab from the film and, in Photoshop, transformed the logo on the tin to read as one of the features. He then created two further tins and the shelf design. The grippers were built in 3D using Infini-D, animating the claws in an appropriate fashion and applying old metal textures created in Photoshop. The two were composited together in After Effects to make it appear that the grabber is lifting the pomade from the shelf.

Above: *For* O Brother, Where Art Thou?, *the menu option subpictures were designed in the style of the movie, in particular the scene depicted in the main menu, an escape from a chain gang. The images here show how they took on the form of crossed tools and how the designer would deliver a subpicture to the DVD author. On the final DVD, the user only sees one button at a time.*

No matter how clever your mechanisms are, try at all times to make the selection process obvious

Matching the interactivity to the theme

If you have the time and resources, you can really make your menu elements aid the interactive nature of the DVD format. Simplest of all methods is the use of button highlights to signify that a user has selected and activated a button. To demonstrate this interaction, designers and applications make use of the subpicture overlay. Subpictures can be employed as simple shapes for functional buttons, or be designed to complement the theme of the DVD. If you want to be more adventurous, and have access to a compositing tool like Adobe After Effects or discreet Combustion, you can make the elements appear animated. On computer-based DVD players, you can also build 'container' or kiosk environments within which to play the content, that give the user the illusion of direct interaction with the DVD content. But no matter how clever your mechanisms are, try at all times to make the selection process obvious and keep the menu as functional as possible.

Taking interaction further

More and more multimedia authoring tools are being developed that allow designers to build interactive environments to control and present DVD content. Macromedia Director MX 2004 has drag and drop components that make it easy to create a DVD playback controller, while the *Event Manager* tool is designed to aid the creation of DVD presentations activities that respond to interaction. Clicking buttons on the menu, for example, could launch animations or link to external webpages. It also allows Macromedia Flash developers to create DVD playback interfaces without requiring any knowledge of Director programming.

Above: The O Brother, Where Art Thou? *menu had to be redesigned for a Special Edition DVD release many months later. This shows the value of leaving room on your menu design for any unforeseen additions. There were more options than hair pomade tins this time around, so the designer decided to use the wall behind to add two more options for a music video and, appropriately enough, a poster that linked to footage from a live concert.*

Although interactive programing is highly useful for educational purposes, such as training DVDs, and as a tool for developing promotional media, your audience will need a computer to make use of it. What's more the disc as a whole will be unusable in consumer DVD players. The key advantage in taking this route, however, is that the capacity for designing interactive elements is comparable to that found in Web design.

Providing access

Generally speaking. you should do whatever you can when designing your menu to make the user experience as smooth as possible, giving your audience quick access to the parts of the DVD they really want to see. You can ensure that navigation is as simple as possible by predefining the navigation of the buttons on the remote control. When setting up your buttons, you have the option to choose to auto assign the button navigation to follow a preset path (also known as automatic routing). However, you may want to customize the button route to select non-sequential buttons to give quicker access to content, so most authoring packages allow you to turn off the auto-route or auto-assign buttons and use manual tools instead. Note that, if you are dealing with any adult content, you may want to control access, by locking part of your audience out of some or all of the content (*see page 177*)

When designing buttons over graphics, be careful not to make the selection area for the button too small, or make it overlap with the selection area of a neighbouring button.

Button over video

As we've discussed elsewhere, designers can also use chapter markers to provide quick access to content from the menu or within content. By assigning buttons to jump to the chapter markers in your content stream, you can provide quick access to the most relevant information for your audience – the key parts of your portfolios for example, or the vows at a wedding ceremony.

You might want to display or place these buttons over the video itself, in which case you can use a button highlight marker. This is configured as part of the subtitle layer and as such shares all its limitations and qualities. The process is known as assigning 'buttons over video' and is available in most professional DVD authoring packages. As well as allowing viewers to jump directly to content elsewhere on the DVD, you can also set the button 'end action' to return to where you started from or move to another marker altogether.

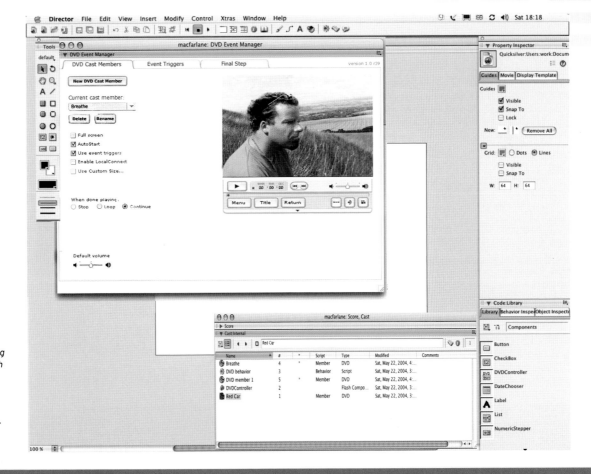

Right: *Macromedia Director MX 2004 provides an authoring environment in which you can design and add menu elements that provide a much higher level of interactivity for your DVD when used on a computer.*

Making sure your DVD is user-friendly

You want to make your DVD as user-friendly as you can, for all possible audiences. A good way to check is to test it to make sure that it actually works. We'll discuss in this section the procedures you should follow and the conventions you should be aware of when preparing to launch your masterpiece on an unsuspecting world.

Authoring an assistive DVD

As well as adhering to the design basics when creating menus, you should pay special attention to any potential usability problems. You may not be designing DVDs for a blockbuster movie release that's going to be seen by millions, but your audience may still include some hard of hearing or visually impaired users. Of course, it's wise to think about these issues at the earliest part of the design process.

When considering a visually impaired audience, you need to pay close attention to colour and font legibility. Some otherwise sighted users may experience difficulty in distinguishing between colour combinations used for button highlights, for example. It is possible to develop menus with single button access to turn on or off disabled access at the highest level, and this switch could be scripted to respond to a key combination on the remote control. As there is no common standard defined within the DVD

Below: *Studio Pro allows you to create a simulation of how your project will appear at any time. It includes playback controls, which replicate the remote control handset on DVD players, and can be customized in the same way. Information about menu elements and their settings can also be displayed in the simulator. Other professional DVD authoring applications have similar preview modes.*

industry for this button sequence on the remote, it's wise to avoid using interactive interfaces that demand the user to respond to a sequence of different visual prompts each time.

An audio menu that guides the user to the content is another option you can build into your authoring process to help viewers who are visually impaired. But while this may be useful, the content on the disc may not be similarly assisted. There are also limitations to this kind of navigation, and the DVD industry again lacks a standard implementation procedure. The DVD specification only allows you to link to one audio file in each menu, so some creative thinking is necessary to create a truly useful solution. You also need to make the user aware that there is an audio navigation addition to the menu, so burying the option deep in a nest of language setting and audio menus with only visual access is obviously counterproductive. A simple, straightforward menu design with audio options at the highest level is advisable.

For physically disabled users, you can make sure that the navigation is as simple as possible by predefining the navigation of the buttons on the remote control (see Providing access, page 174).

Simulators and previews

When all your footage is in place, your buttons are linked and your menu is complete, you need to test it. Most authoring packages include some kind of simulator to carry out this task as it is an essential part of the process. You need to see if your buttons actually work, if the quality of video, audio, and graphics in your menus and on the DVD are up to scratch, and if your transitions are working as planned.

Access and parental control

Most DVD authoring packages have tools to support the imposition of a parental lockout for possibly unsuitable content. If you are creating a commercial DVD that could offend parts of your audience, you have to build this feature into your authoring process. Be aware that different countries have different ideas of what is acceptable, or even legal, to show on screen. If you are preparing a commercial disc that may be seen abroad, it is only common sense to investigate beforehand what may constitute an offence in the countries concerned.

DVD players use the System Parameter Registers (SPRM) levels 12 and 13 to store the status of parental management features. SPRM 12 stores the country code for the player's parental management feature, while SPRM 13 holds the value of the ratings system – PG has a value of 3, a disc with rating R has a value of 6, and so on. The user can adjust the rating level of the player and any passwords using the onscreen setup menu of the DVD player itself.

In those professional packages that support scripting, you can write a script that checks if the current setting of the DVD player is lower than the rating you have assigned for the DVD. In these cases, the player can be set to ignore the DVD and not play the disc or only give access to certain parts of the content. The control can be unlocked by entering a password preset by the author.

DVDs have the facility to offer alternative versions of content (see pages 166-169) and this function can also be used for parental control purposes. A disc with a high parental control rating may branch seamlessly to the alternate streams, depending on the level set for the player. Again, a password can be set to unlock the protected content.

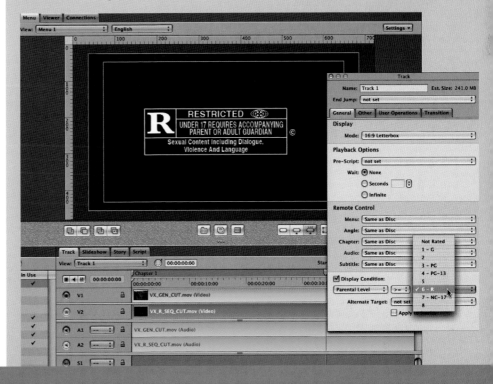

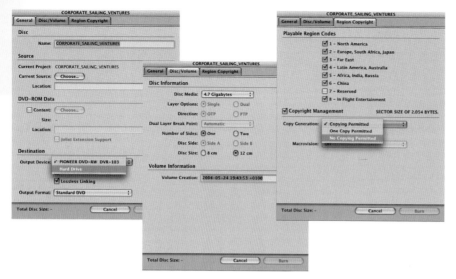

As well as using the simulator in your application and the computer's DVD player to run emulations, it is wise to burn a test version of the DVD before sending it out to clients, family, and friends. This extended view of the Build/Format menu settings in DVD studio Pro shows the large amount of customizable properties available in the Apple authoring application. Other professional tools have a similar range of output options.

Things to remember before you burn

Be sure to have set the correct size, type, and format (double-sided, DVD-5, DVD-9, etc.) for your disc before building the project. Make sure the region coding is correct, and set to 0 if you want the disc to play anywhere. This is only really applicable if you are preparing the disc for replication, as projects written directly to DVD-R will have all regions enabled. If you are preparing the DVD for replication and you worry about copies being made of your content, turn on copy protection – the most common are Content Scrambling System (CSS) and Macrovision – that will encrypt your DVD while authoring. Another type of protection is CGMS, which sets a restriction on the amount of copies that can be made from an encrypted DVD. Copy protection is off by default and only works if you are writing the project to a digital linear tape (DLT) before replication.

Building the DVD

Once you are satisfied, and have also set the disc size, copy protection, and region coding, if applicable, you can go ahead and build the DVD file. This is the term used for creating the VIDEO_TS (video tile set) folder that will go on your DVD disc. All your data (video, audio, subpictures, and program chains) are multiplexed together into video object (VOB) files, each up to 1GB in size and stored in the VIDEO_TS folder. From here, you can emulate the finished DVD using your DVD player software. If all is working fine, you can burn the project to a test DVD.

Burning the disc

Something else to consider at this stage is the disc format on which to burn the project. Burning your own DVD content onto commercially available, recordable DVD discs does not involve the same process as used in the mass replication of DVDs for movies or music video purposes. The commercially available

format most used for burning is DVD-R for General, while replication plants use the more expensive and restrictive DVD-R for Authoring format. For testing, use DVD-RW or DVD+RW discs, if possible, as this allows for reuse. These formats are also less forgiving than DVD-R for General, so if these play well, the project will probably work with the more stable DVD-R format.

To begin, select Build or a similar command from your application menu. This will start a process whereby the computer checks all the links between files in your project, highlighting those that require fixing. Once you have gone back and fixed the links, you can choose parameters such as the write speed, initial disc settings, the number of copies to create, and the destination, whether you have a DVD recorder or a DLT device – all before you go ahead and burn. Use brand name media whenever possible, as inferior makes, while considerably less expensive, may cause problems and repeat testing.

Left: *You need to check for missing or unassigned links in your project before you build it. You can do this automatically at build time with applications such as Adobe Encore DVD, or run a check at any time during your project.*

Testing the DVD

You need to be sure that everyone will be able to play your DVD. Play the test disc in both your home DVD player and on your computer DVD player. If possible, use a friend's DVD player as an additional test machine and try to test the disc on both a Mac and PC, especially if you are including DVD-ROM content or Web links on the disc.

Check for optimum quality playback of video, audio, and graphics on each test platform. Look out for skipped frames, pauses, stuttering, or digital artifacts in the video, as well as noise, audible pops, or dropouts in the sound.

Make sure all the navigation works on your carefully constructed menu system and all links and buttons perform in exactly the way they should.

If any problems do show up, try rechecking using the simulator again and burn the test disc at the lowest speed supported by your DVD recorder. If there are specific audio or video problems such as dropouts or pauses, try re-encoding using a low to medium bit rate for the video.

Once testing is complete and you are satisfied, you can go ahead and write your project to DVD-R for final

Fat Boy Slim - Big Beach Boutique II

When DVD design company The Pavement were commissioned to design and author a DVD covering an open-air beach concert by leading British DJ Fat Boy Slim, they decided the best way to approach the task was to get closely involved with the event.

A close-up look at the menu

A stylized cloud layer animates in the background. These fast-moving clouds add a surreal sense of magic to the menu to help capture the excitement of the event.

A layer of boats bobs in the background, as though their occupants want to join in the fun of the concert. As the boats move quite a way during the 20-second menu sequence, the whole image flares up at the end of the loop to disguise the fact that they are re-set in their starting positions.

The seaside coin-operated telescope allows the DVD user to navigate to the disc's submenus. By interacting with the camera, the user feels immersed in the concert's environment. The Fat Boy Slim logo has been added to the camera body to help brand the disc's menu.

A movie of a dancing crowd plays on a layer behind the camera's foreground layer. Animated After Effects spotlights sweep back and forth over the crowd to add more movement, texture, and detail to the menu.

The main menu is a montage of various photographic and video elements shot on location, which were composited together in After Effects. It is designed to make you feel that you are actually at the concert.

To enhance the sense of participation, the designers used sound in the menu. While the menu loops we hear the cheering crowd and music playing in the distance. To stop the looping menu from jarring abruptly, the sound is faded up at the start of the loop and down at the end.

Researching the location

To reflect the feel of the live event, The Pavement based the design around the concert's location. This required the team to take a trip to the British seaside resort of Brighton. On the day before, they photographed many of the town's beach-location icons, including the telescopes used to look out at the sea, and the fairground rides, games, and sideshows found on the famous Brighton Pier. This gave them a variety of elements to use in the final menus.

As well as capturing still elements, the crew also took DV cameras and filmed the construction of the stage, the helicopters flying overhead, and shots of the concert itself with thousands of people dancing on the beach. All of these were brought together to create a lively, animated menu that perfectly captures the excitement and energy of the event. The live footage was also used to create several transition movies and some extras for the disc, including a 'Making Of' movie.

Around a quarter of a million people attended the Brighton concert. As a big event with a huge audience, it deserved a big DVD. In their clever use of menu design, this is exactly what The Pavement delivered.

Right: *When the disc is first inserted, a short introduction movie plays to lead the viewer to the main menu. The image is distorted, as though the viewer is looking through the lens of the telescope.*

Below: *The camera zooms out from the lens of the telescope to reveal the beach party in full flow. As we zoom out of the lens, the telescope tilts to its default position.*

Left: *The interactive telescope theme continues throughout the DVD's menus and submenus, effectively anchoring the disc's various menu elements.*

Left: *The designers at The Pavement spent a great deal of time adding tiny details to the DVD's menu, like using After Effects to put post-production camera flashes in the crowd. This kind of attention to detail adds a glossy, professional finish to the disc.*

Below: *Once the main menu has appeared, the DVD user is free to explore the contents of the disc. Selecting each menu option with the DVD remote brings up a red subpicture, which is overlaid on the telescope's menu text.*

Right: *Clicking on the Play icon on the telescope triggers a seamless transition movie that shows the camera rapidly panning left, away from the telescope. This indicates that we have made a decision and are off to see Fat Boy Slim in action.*

Below: *The menu then pans left from the telescope and the movie becomes a blur. There's a quick edit in the whip pan where we cut to a fast dolly shot, giving us the sensation that we are racing through the crowd towards the heart of the concert.*

Left: *Finally, we rush up to the main stage, where Fat Boy Slim can be seen from behind, mixing his records to the delight of the crowd. The transition movie fades rapidly to black and the main DVD recording of the concert begins to play. The sequence lasts 8 seconds, which could seem too long. The speeded-up video footage in the sequence helps make it seem shorter.*

Introducing the extras

The Fat Boy Slim DVD is more than just a record of a pop concert. It's an interactive and immersive experience thanks to the menu design. Let's take a closer look at some of its innovative menu features.

Right: *The extras menu has two arrows to encourage the user to navigate left or right. There's also an 'Easter egg' option that carries no clues as to its existence or location. If the user presses the up option on their remote while in the Extras submenu, they activate an invisible link that triggers another transition movie. The telescope tilts up to show video footage of a helicopter, which was shot by The Pavement on location at Brighton.*

Left: *The user isn't left without some guidance, as this would be frustrating. Subtle animated arrows rotate to the left and right of the telescope's field of view, giving a hint for the DVD user to select the left or right buttons on their remote. The arrows are rotated on a separate layer in After Effects, and are combined with the other layered components like the boat movie. This Extras submenu is unusual because it doesn't contain any subpictures to indicate that a menu option has been selected. It works on a more intuitive level, as the user only has the animated arrow menu elements to guide them.*

Right: *By clicking right on the remote, the user triggers a transition movie of a telescope pan that takes them to the DJ Request menu. Here they can take control of DJ Fat Boy Slim's playlist by clicking on the track numbers to rearrange the track order. As a new track is added, a new record appears in the record box. Clicking on Play then plays the disc's music tracks in the order they have been selected. This menu element gives the user greater control of how they interact with the disc's content and is another example of its innovation.*

Left: *The code needed to access extra footage is not found within the DVD packaging, as The Pavement's Andy Evans explains: 'You have to go to the website to get it, so the DVD promotes the Web and vice versa, which is a nice little marketing tool.'*

Seaside games

The DVD medium is popular because it allows the user more options than just watching a piece of video. The Pavement was eager to push the boundaries. This is why they made sure that they were involved before, during, and after the Fat Boy Slim footage was recorded, so that they could incorporate as much of the live event as possible into their design. Being on location allowed them to create some unique extras for the disc, as Andy Evans explains: 'What we've got is two bits of footage. We've got the 'making of' which we shot. We were down there shooting backstage as well. And the other extra is the photo gallery. The guys went around in the crowd with Polaroid cameras and clearance forms. The fans wrote a little message to Fat Boy in the white bit of the Polaroid.'

Fans who were at the concert can buy the DVD with the hope of seeing their picture, but they have to win a game first! Clicking left in the Extras menu accesses the DVD's games. Again, no subpicture appears when you use the remote. You just go straight to the next menu. This speeds up user interaction with the disc's contents, as you don't need to select then activate a button to jump from one menu to another.

Dolphin Derby

The pier games on the DVD are designed to give you the experience of Brighton. To play the Dolphin Derby, you choose a dolphin and the game plays randomly. If you win, a transition movie of a roller coaster plays before showing you the specially shot 'Making Of' footage of the concert.

Right: *The Pavement designed a win and a lose screen. The lose screen includes a link to let you play again.*

Right: *The DVD's Dolphin Derby game is designed to mimic a game that is found on Brighton Pier. The dolphins and waves are layered and animated in After Effects.*

Left: *The target game features multiple animated layers put together in After Effects. Random movies play in which Fat Boy 'pops up'. A target-shaped subpicture can be moved over the target and activated by pressing enter.*

Bottom left: *When a target is 'hit', it triggers a movie of Fat Boy exploding, complete with bits of 3D debris.*

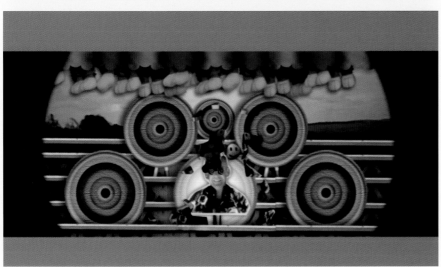

The second game designed and created by The Pavement is more interactive. Andy talks us through it: 'What happens is Fat Boy pops up and you have to use the navigation controls on the remote to shoot him. To shoot him you have to hit enter. If you win, you see the photo gallery. I can never win this game when I'm demonstrating the disc. The faster players are much easier to use.'

Andy's last comment points to the constraints of DVD hardware. To get our game screenshots for this book, we used a computer with a mouse, which was a much easier way to select the relevant target than using a remote. When designing games, don't forget the limitations of the TV remote, which is what most people will be using to access DVD content.

The designers were involved before, during, and after the Fat Boy Slim footage was recorded so that they could incorporate as much of the live event as possible into their design.

glossary

Action-Safe

The standardized central portion of a PAL or NTSC television screen in which any action should be clearly visible and free from excess distortion, regardless of the age, make, or model of the set being watched.

Alpha Channel/Alpha Matte

A feature used by certain applications to control what parts of an image will appear transparent when viewed or rendered. This enables any graphic elements, such as buttons or subpictures, to be created with transparent backgrounds, so that an image placed behind will show through.

Artefact

A visual disturbance of an image, usually an area of ugly colour blocks, caused by flaws in the image-capture or storage systems.

Aspect Ratio

The ratio of the width of a picture to its height. The conventional video and TV aspect ratio is 4:3, but this is rapidly being replaced by a 16:9 widescreen ratio.

Authoring

The process of coding and burning a set of files to a CD or DVD, complete with menus or an interface to control how a user can interact with them. In the case of DVD, authoring means getting all the video, audio and still image data on the disc and connecting it all together via menus.

Broadcast Legal

The strict (but loosening) code of practice that only permits certain chrominance and luminance values in a video signal. This helps maintain the quality and consistency of broadcast TV signals across the full variety of TV sets.

Channels

In digital imaging, the colour information in an image or video signal is split into separate channels – red, green, and blue for screen, or cyan, magenta, yellow, and black for print. These channels can be edited or operated on independently, and additional channels (alpha channels) can be added to control selections or transparency.

Chapter

A segment of video on a DVD disc consisting of one or more VOB files. Chapters are normally used to break a movie down into sensible chunks. This makes it easier for the viewer to navigate forwards or backwards to the portion they want to watch.

Chapter Marker

Markers placed on the timeline of a DVD movie to delineate the beginning or end of a chapter.

Chrominance

The colour values of an image, measured in RGB levels.

Decode

The process of converting digital data into an image or audio/video stream.

De-Interlace

The process of combining the two fields of a video 'frame' into a single frame. This combats the lines or blurring that can become noticeable when a still frame is grabbed from an interlaced video source.

chapter markers

© TCFHE Ltd.

© TCFHE Ltd.

Dissolve

Dissolve

An audio/video transition that mixes two shots through the lowering of opacity on the first shot combined with a simultaneous raising of opacity on the second.

Dolby 5.1

Also known as AC3 or Dolby Digital, this is the most common standard of surround audio used by commercial DVDs, with the sound converted into five signals for two front, two rear and one centre dialogue speaker, plus a subwoofer to boost the bass.

DTS

An alternative to Dolby 5.1, DTS supplies a form of 5.1 surround audio with a larger dynamic range, making it arguably of higher quality.

DVD

Digital Versatile Disc. High capacity development of the Compact Disc, allowing storage of up to 8.5GB of data on a dual-layer disc. This capacity, combined with MPEG-2 video compression and the DVD-Video standard, has made DVD an ideal choice for home video playback, and the main standard for commercial video releases.

DVD+RW

A rewritable DVD standard promoted by Sony, Philips, and others, allowing storage of up to 4.7GB of data, or up to 8.5GB on a dual-layer, write-once DVD+R disc.

DVD-ROM

A DVD or a section of a DVD used to store data for computer use. On a commercial DVD, a section might be given over to content that can only be accessed from computer, including web links, games, or additional production notes and sketches.

DVD-RW

The official rewritable DVD standard of the DVD alliance, as promoted by Pioneer, Apple and others, allowing storage of up to 4.7GB of data on a rewritable disc, or up to 8.5GB on a dual-layer, write-once DVD-R disc.

Encoder

A programme that converts digital data or an analogue signal into the digital data required by a certain format. For example, converting DV video to MPEG-2 for DVD.

Field

One of the two parts of an image (upper or lower) that a television signal interlaces to create an illusion of the complete frame.

Font

A complete typeface, consisting of a full range of letter shapes and punctuation marks, all sharing a common look and style.

Interlacing

The process whereby a conventional CRT television produces an image from two frames, one comprising the odd horizontal lines and one comprising the even horizontal lines, alternating between them at 60 frames per second (in NTSC) to create the illusion of a single image updating at 30 frames per second.

JPEG

Joint Photographic Experts Group - a special interest group set up by figures in the photographic and digital imaging industries for the creation of standard file formats for photographic images. However, the term JPEG is mainly used to describe the widely-used compressed file format that bears the group's name. The JPEG format allows for controllable degrees of compression, enabling the user to balance image-quality against file-size according to the purpose of the file.

Keyframe

A concept borrowed from traditional animation, where a lead artist would draw the most important frames of a sequence, then junior artists would create the in-between frames. In digital video, keyframes are used to control an effect or animation. The user sets a keyframe, alters the values of parameters or the position of an element, then sets a new keyframe. The program then calculates the effects on frames in-between, and renders them accordingly.

Layers

A feature taken from image-editing programs, such as Photoshop, but now also applied to video. Layers work like transparent acetate sheets to which video or still images are assigned. Layers can be made more or less transparent, deleteted, or have their order changed to alter compositions or montage elements together into a seamless whole.

Luminance

The amount of light attributed to a pixel or image, effectively controlling its brightness.

MPEG2

File compression standard for digital video, set by the Motion Pictures Expert Group, principally for use in the DVD format.

NLE

A digital editing system, which allows a movie to be assembled in any order, so that shots can be shuffled or repositioned and effects or transitions added at will, without needing to work through the film sequentially. Non-linear editing is a more flexible and intuitive process than traditional film editing or linear video editing.

NTSC (National Television Standards Committee)

The TV standard used by the USA, Canada, Japan, and many other countries in South America and the Pacific region. NTSC uses 525 lines made up of two interlaced fields scanned at 29.97 frames per second or 59.94 fields per second.

Opacity

A percentage attribute given to a video clip, an image, or any part of an image, in order to control its level of transparency.

PAL

Phase Alternation Line. The standard TV display format for the UK, most European countries, Australia, New Zealand, and some others. PAL uses a 625 line display, made up of two interlaced fields which each refresh 25 times per second for a 50 frames per second total.

PGC

Program Chain. The simple programs used within the DVD-Video standard to control the operation of the disc, including its menus, the sequencing of chapters, the playback of audio, and access and permissions.

PSD

Image file-format created by Adobe for use in Photoshop. The PSD format stores a wide range of information beyond the pixel data, including layers and channels. This enables more flexibility should you want to return to an image and re-edit it later on. Some DVD authoring programs are able to work directly with layered PSD files, enabling menu designers to create layouts in Photoshop, then import them into an authoring program to set up the mechanics of the menu.

Render

The digital process of converting data and a set of instructions into a finished still or moving image. This might be video (footage transformed with effects, cuts, and transitions), a 3D animation (scene data rendered with lights and textures), or a still photograph (the original photo with a complex effect applied to it).

Rollover

In web design, a button which responds when the pointer crosses over it, usually via a change of shape or colour, to give the user visual feedback. DVD menus don't support the same effect, but can do something similar via sub-pictures.

Saturation

The strength of colour in a colour video signal.

SPRM

System Parameter Registers. 24 built-in variables in the standard DVD-Video player specification that store the

subpictures

current player settings. These can then be accessed by program chains to control the behaviour of a DVD disc during playback.

Storyboard
Originally a frame-by-frame diagram of a movie sequence, storyboards are also used to plan our a menu structure, screen by screen.

Subpicture
Every DVD track can contain up to 32 subpicture tracks, which allow simple text or graphics in one of four colours to overlay the video. These subpictures are used in menus to create graphics or highlights for button selection, or as subtitles or captions while the video content is playing.

Template
A ready-made project containing all the fundamental elements, styled for a particular purpose, such as a wedding video or corporate training.

A template can usually be tweaked to fit the needs of an individual production.

Thumbnail
A smaller, low-resolution version of an image or video clip, usually used to identify and select the full-size, high-resolution version.

Timeline
A single or multitrack line representing the length of video and audio clips during editing in chronological order. Clips can be dragged to the *Timeline*, arranged in order, cut, and extended.

Title-Safe
A standard area within a PAL or NTSC television screen in which any titles will display without any cropping or excess distortion.

Transcode
To take video or audio encoded in one format and re-encode it to another.

Transition
A change from one image or video clip to another, using an animated effect or simulated optical effect instead of a straight cut.

VOB
Video Object file. A file containing all the video and audio data for a sequence of the movie that will be contained on the DVD.

template

index and acknowledgments

Thanks to the following for
sharing their time and DVD
design skills

Julian Day
Keri Elmsly
Andy Evans
Kathryn Davey
Tim Long
Lloyd Shaer

Thanks to **Justin** and **Neil**
from **Zero Balance** for use of
their Sci-Fi short, *They Came
For a Day.*

Thanks to **Mark Warner**,
Luke Tilly, **Suzanne Elston**,
and all at Abbey Road Interactive
for their help.

DVD Menu images are used
with the kind permission of
EMI, Twentieth Century Fox
Home Entertainment, Universal,
Carlton, Aardman Animations,
and Momentum Pictures. All
images used for critical and
illustrative purposes only. All
copyright remains with the
respective holders.

www.ilex-press.com
www.web-linked.com

ilex-press.com is the home of all things ILEX. Don't forget to visit our website for news on the latest ILEX books, tutorials, competitions, give-aways and online resources to get the best out of your ILEX books.

Get 20% off ILEX books
All purchases through the ILEX online bookstore will automatically save you 20% off the cover price.

Join our email list
Sign up for the ILEX eNewsletter and get up-to-the-minute news on ILEX books, authors, promotions and speaker events.

Free online tutorials
Each month we'll be featuring free tutorials from the latest ILEX titles, so if you are looking for useful tips for improving your workflow or want to try your hand at creating impressive digital art, then check out our tutorials section.

Monthly giveaways
We will be giving away free copies of our latest books to registered members every month. Sign up today, and you could be one of the lucky few to receive a free ILEX book.

Expert advice in the forum
Visit the online forum and share expertise with your peers, or ask ILEX authors and experts for advice on creative and technical issues.

Join our affiliate programme
If you run a website, newsgroup or online gallery, become an ILEX affiliate and earn 10% referral fees for books sold through links to our site.

web-linked.com is a unique online resource for every ILEX book. Make sure you visit the web-linked site for this book **www.dvdmuk.web-linked.com** to access useful links and download source files to get the most out of your purchase. You'll find directories of websites and organizations that will help you develop your knowledge and skills, and you can follow step-by-step tutorials in the books using the original artwork used by our authors.